CONSERVATION: NOW OR NEVER

Also by Nicholas Roosevelt

THEODORE ROOSEVELT: The Man as I Knew Him

A FRONT ROW SEAT

A NEW BIRTH OF FREEDOM

CREATIVE COOKING

Conservation:
Now or Never

NICHOLAS ROOSEVELT

DODD, MEAD & COMPANY

NEW YORK

Second Printing

Copyright © 1970 by Nicholas Roosevelt

All rights reserved

No part of this book may be reproduced in any form without permission in writing from the publisher

Library of Congress Catalog Card Number: 74-105294
Printed in the United States of America
by The Cornwall Press, Inc., Cornwall, N. Y.

ACKNOWLEDGMENTS

To list all who helped me appraise aspects of conservation discussed in this book would fill pages. But to three men I am particularly indebted for sound guidance in shaping the book's contents. Two of the three, Horace M. Albright and Newton B. Drury, each served for years as director of the National Park Service. The third, DeWitt Nelson, was state forester of California and director of the state's Department of Conservation. I am grateful for their help and treasure their friendship.

N. R.

FOREWORD

This book deals with saving scenic resources. It is based on a half century of active interest in conservation, and on talks with many conservationists about their aims and frustrations. I have by-passed problems of urban parks and playgrounds because my contacts with them have been few. So also, even though I am sure that water and air pollution present the greatest threats to the survival of civilization next to the misuse of atomic power, I have omitted them because I lack the technical and legal background to discuss how they can be controlled.

Instead, I show how concepts of conservation have changed since President Theodore Roosevelt focalized nation-wide attention on the subject in the early 1900s, and give case histories of the forces working for and against conservation. The struggle will intensify as the rapid growth of population increases the already keen rivalry for land. What is not soon set aside for parks and recreation, or protected as "open space," will be forever lost for conservation.

—NICHOLAS ROOSEVELT

Big Sur, California

CONTENTS

Foreword   vii

1. LESS LAND FOR MORE PEOPLE   1

2. TO USE OR TO KEEP?   12

3. PARADISE LOST   26

4. TRADING LAND FOR TREES   39

5. CATTLE VS. VISITORS   51

6. MULTIPLE USE OF FORESTS   61

7. WHAT WILDERNESS?   72

8. FIGHTING FOREST FIRES   84

9. UNCLE SAM, LANDLORD   97

10. WANTED: REGIONAL PARKS   106

11. OREGON CAPITALIZES SCENERY   114

12. RURAL PARKS FOR CITY PEOPLE   129

13. IOWA POINTS THE WAY   144

14. NEW HAMPSHIRE SAVES BEAUTY   155

ix

15. MAKE STRAIGHT A HIGHWAY 171

16. WANTED: MORE GIANTS 185

17. STORMING STORM KING 197

18. A COUNTY SAVES A COAST 209

19. WHAT LIES AHEAD 224

Index 233

CONSERVATION: NOW OR NEVER

LESS LAND FOR MORE PEOPLE

WHEN the word "conservation" came into use around 1900 it implied saving natural resources on Federal lands for future, rather than current, consumption. In modern phraseology the resources were to be put in the deep freeze.

Had anyone then suggested that scenery was among the most valuable of our natural resources, only a few dreamers would have understood. Today we know better. Although conservation has many objectives, these call for protection of areas of exceptional natural beauty from destruction or severe mutilation by logging, stripping, draining, damming, and flooding, or by ramming freeways through them with mechanically and unimaginatively cleared rights-of-way. After decades of confused thinking we see at last that scenery is limited in extent, irreplaceable and invaluable.

Where the original theory of conservation of natural resources was based on ultimate use and consumption, today's concept of conservation centers on use without consumption or destruction—use through enabling an increasing number of visitors to enjoy the natural beauties of areas that have been set aside, and, in pleasant surroundings, to indulge in forms of recreation as varied as motoring for pleasure, boating, swimming, hiking, skiing, fishing, and camping. It is based on the fact that millions today seek escape from the drabness of overcrowded living and working conditions by engaging in these activities, and have the means to do so. Their use of parks and recreation areas does not impair or consume the natural resources of the areas.

Necessarily the combination of use with preservation presents administrative problems. But by skilled planning of the location and structure of roads, trails, campgrounds, picnic areas, viewpoints, and other conveniences for visitors large sections of parks and recreation areas can be kept in a state of nature. Most visitors use the roads and trails and the designated picnic and camp grounds. Foresight and imagination on the part of park administrators enable them to anticipate the kinds of viewpoints and overlooks that visitors will enjoy and to build new trails accordingly. Experience has shown that repeated trampling of an area not only injures its natural cover but even can kill the feeding roots of big trees. This has happened in parts of the Sequoia and the Yosemite National Parks. But the superintendents early learned that this sort of damage could be lessened by the use of wide boardwalks, or of paths covered with a deep layer of chipped bark, wherever the public tended to stray. When such facilities exist most visitors respect the "keep off" signs.

I remember talking about this problem forty years ago with the able and engaging superintendent of Sequoia National Park, Colonel John R. White, formerly of the Philippine constabulary. A Britisher by birth, he had lived most of his life in the United States. After a tour of duty in the Philippines during the American occupation of those islands, he joined the National Park Service and by his combination of shrewdness, hardheadedness and kindliness, he guided wisely the early development of the Sequoia National Park for visitors.

Believing that preservation and use were not incompatible Colonel White built trails to scenic sectors of the park which could not be reached by road. But he found that some of the trails, while safe for seasoned hikers and climbers, could overtax inexperienced visitors. These trails he closed to the general public. But the inevitable happened. A visitor complained to his congressman that he had been denied the use of a trail of his choice in the Sequoia National Park. The congressman took it up with the director of the National Park Service in Washington. Doubtless the congressman metaphorically beat his breast as he pointed out that the national parks belonged to the people—all the people—and that therefore anyone had a right to go wherever he wished. Reluctantly the head of the National Park Service passed along the protest to Colonel White. The Colonel, wise in the ways of politicians and the public, reopened the trails, thus placating the politician, but rebuilt the first mile of these trails and saw to it that the new sections were laid out with so many rough stretches difficult to get over that the hikers whom he wished to keep out soon sought easier trails.

This kind of administrative solution shows the interrelationship between effective preservation and reasonable use. I mention it here because it helps to clarify the multiple goals of conservation. More areas should be managed for the protection of rare kinds of wildlife. The farther these areas are from thickly populated centers the easier will it be to exclude trespassers. More areas should be set aside as particularly interesting samples of geology. Still other areas must be preserved in order to protect more spectacular examples. Among these are watersheds upstream from the groves of coast redwoods in California, which are needed not because of their inherent scenic or forest values but because, if these watersheds are logged, erosion can cause disastrous effects downstream. A notable example is the damage to the magnificent coast redwoods in the Rockefeller Forest in the Bull Creek area by the erosion which followed the unregulated logging on privately owned timber lands along the upper reaches of Bull Creek.

Today there is an urgency about conservation that did not exist in the days of Gifford Pinchot and Theodore Roosevelt—urgency because unless lands suitable for esthetic enjoyment and recreation are protected they will be exploited for commercial purposes and thus will be forever lost for conservation. Never has there been such fierce rivalry for land on the part of contenders who have legitimate but mutually conflicting aims. Land is wanted for offices, warehouses, and factories; for homes; for supermarkets and parking lots; for highways and drive-in motion picture theaters; for the expansion of cities and towns. It is obvious that new plans to set aside recreation areas compete with these and similar land uses.

Conservation is now a major concern of many powerful and effective organizations, such as the American Forestry Association, the Audubon Society, the Wilderness Society, the Izaak Walton League, the Save-the-Redwoods League. The cause is supported by foundations, and by an army of men and women devoted to one or another of the multiple goals of conservation. Governments will continue to act as coordinators, protectors, and administrators, but the impetus for the setting aside of new sites will have to come from dedicated conservationists. Theirs has been—and will remain—the task of dramatizing and publicizing objectives.

Fortunately, if you scratch a conservationist you are likely to find a crusader under the skin. Among conservationists are artists and dreamers and hardy hikers and mountaineers; hunters and fishermen; passionate protectors of wildlife; men and women who love natural beauty and who want to save some, at least, of the most spectacular remnants of the nation's scenic heritage. Most conservationists have a favorite objective—saving redwoods, or wilderness areas, or the Everglades, or birds, or buffaloes. A friend of mine who has been one of the most effective workers in the overall field of conservation for years has two special concerns—to protect sea otters and mountain lions. Some conservationists speak of themselves as "preservationists," by which label they imply that they want to preserve areas as they now are and close them forever to the public. Others believe in multiple use, which is anathema to preservationists because it includes commercial exploitation of portions of Federally owned lands. Some want to save birds—notably ducks—for hunters to kill, whereas many of their fellow conservationists would gladly see all hunters killed if this would keep the skies dark with ducks forevermore. Members of the Audubon Society are said to dream of the time when the now-extinct passenger pigeons were so numerous in the Eastern forests that their weight broke down even large limbs of big trees on which they roosted at night. Some conservationists have a passion for saving wildlife, whether in Africa, Argentina, Australia or Alaska, whereas others take a narrow nationalist view of wildlife and are glad to give to a fund to protect the Gila monsters on the Arizona desert but want bushmen to look after their own fauna "down under" and care nothing about what the Eskimos do with the seals in the Arctic. When conservationists meet, each talks loudly about his own special interest and takes it for granted that no one will listen. But when a conservation cause needs help, conservationists go to bat gladly and effectively.

All of which suggests that among conservationists are some of the most effective rugged individualists who ever worked together towards a common goal. I have known many in the last fifty years and have admired their dedication to causes dear to their hearts. A few held public office. Others guided conservation organizations. Some raised money for specific conservation goals. Still others capitalized friendship with journalists and politicians to win support for conservation causes. Of necessity those in government bureaus had to specialize. Members of the National Park Service had—and have —little time for anything but park problems. The work of men in the U. S. Forest Service includes involvement in Job Corps programs, Rural Area Development projects, conservation education with schools, and similar activities. Community and county leaders struggling to enlarge local and regional parks spend much time on jurisdictional problems and in fighting local obstructionists.

Officials of all government levels are restricted in scope by the fact that each bureau acts under its own statutes and regulations. Federal agencies handling aspects of the conservation of natural resources are not under a single government department. The U. S. Forest Service is part of the Department of Agriculture, and the National Park Service is under the Department of the Interior, and, to paraphrase the words of Rudyard Kipling: "Never the twain can meet." The duties of each have been fixed without regard to those of the other.

The same is true of policies. The Forest Service goes in for multiple use, which permits lumbering, mining, and camping on Forest lands, whereas the Park Service excludes all commercial use of parks, except leases to concessionaires who furnish services to visitors. State departments of parks and of recreation are often out of touch with each other, and rarely meet their counterparts in the Federal government. Most counties interested in recreation had to pay their own way in the development of recreational projects until Federal financial aid allocated through the states was made available to them in 1965. Jurisdictional fragmentation was an integral part of the American political system.

I suspect that among the ties uniting workers in fields of conservation is awareness that the nation has destroyed much of its scenic heritage, and determination to control the remnants for the pleasure of future generations. Waste was a by-product of the winning of the wilderness—particularly in the states south and east of the Great Plains, where no one could make a living from a farm without first clearing the trees off the land. The ordeal of carving out a homestead with his own hands convinced each pioneer that he had a right to do as he wished with his land. If a stream crossed it he used the water not only for domestic and agricultural purposes but also to carry away the wastes of his farm and home. If he had a sawmill and chose to dump sawdust in the stream that powered his mill no one stopped him. If he enlarged the mill, he continued the practice. With the spread of industrial plants, many of which also disposed of waste in nearby streams, rivers became—and remain—little more than open drains and sewers, thanks to the congestion of pollutants.

This environmental desecration grew for decades because there was (and still is) little control of, or long-range planning for, land use. Zoning is relatively new and unpopular. Community and regional plans usually arouse strong opposition from local businessmen who dislike regulations of any kind. In fact, the initial reaction of local leaders to suggestions from county, state, or Federal officials about any kind of land use is one of suspicion. People living in a community feel that they know better what that community wants and needs than do outsiders, and it should not be overlooked that to small-town and rural Americans even a county is a large—and almost alien—unit. County officials, in turn, know that they know more about the county's needs and problems than do state officials. When the latter seek to influence county leaders, they intensify resentment against state officials. One of the few common bonds between local and state officials is dislike of any "interference" in state or local affairs by Federal officials, and this despite the fact that except in doling out money to states for specific purposes authorized by acts of Congress interference by the Federal government is rare indeed.

As I look back over a half century of participation in the promotion of conservation projects I realize that this local distrust of county, state, and Federal governments makes the work of supporters of conservation measures difficult. Not even the soundest project that has been devised in the interest of a community, or a county, or even a state can be implemented unless it has grass-roots support. Local leaders can block almost any conservation project for the simple reason that few state legislators will support a project which the voters in their district strongly oppose—as most of them oppose conservation. What is true of state legislators is also true of congressmen, thanks to what in Washington is called "senatorial courtesy"—the system which dictates that if a congressman in whose district a particular project lies refuses to endorse it, his colleagues will be guided by his example. This means that it is easier for local interests to block a proposed conservation measure than it is for nonresident conservationists to induce local legislators or congressmen to support it.

In addition to this automatic local opposition to conservation, there are businesses in the nation which employ lobbyists to fight restrictions on the use of public lands; the setting aside of an area for park and recreation purposes means closing it to possible development by commercial interests. This is nothing new. I remember Theodore Roosevelt telling me in 1913, when we were camping on the North Rim of the Grand Canyon National Monument, that whenever as President he sought to withdraw lands on the public domain from being patented, thus closing them formally to exploitation, he was met by prompt and vigorous opposition from the lobbyists of three groups—the lumber, mining and grazing interests—each of which had long used public lands with little interference, and feared that restrictions placed on one type of activity might serve as precedents for restricting the others. Accordingly, these lobbyists brought pressure to bear on state and local politicians and saw to it that public opposition was loud and effective.

These three groups, strongly supported by groups of sportsmen, are still powerful among the foes of conservation. Often they are supported by lobbyists of the billboard industry, and especially in fighting local conservation projects, by real estate developers. In fairness to these commercial opponents of conservation it should be noted that they are doing as their predecessors did and see no reason why they should be denied chances to profit as others had profited before them. In other words, most of these men are concerned exclusively with making a living and resent restrictions by any level of government on their full freedom of competition.

It is probably just as well that there is no centralized body or organization or branch of government to direct the work of conservationists. Even to establish a list of priorities would be a formidable task because of the lack of criteria by which to rank various proposed projects. Furthermore, the needs of different regions vary as drastically as do the potential areas which might be used for recreation purposes. Even when the obvious generalization is made—that most of the best land for recreational uses is far from the population centers—it does little to clarify thinking. Moreover, there are types of local needs which would be regarded by many conservationists as far from ideal, but which would be enthusiastically welcomed by local residents. A recreation area that appealed to one community might have no appeal to another.

The conclusion is clear that these multiple goals can only be reached through the multiple efforts of many individuals and organizations. Governments, as I have indicated, are the logical custodians and administrators of park and recreation areas. They operate in the name of the community. But the initiative, and most of the support, for conservation goals will have to continue to come from individuals and organizations dedicated to various aspects of the cause of conservation.

Because many goals are still unattained, an examination of case histories may throw useful light on the nature of the problems which individuals and groups will have to face when engaged in conservation crusades. In the following chapters I discuss cases in the pursuit of various objectives, deliberately including failures as well as tales of success. It is my hope that showing methods which conservationists have used, and the nature and origin of the opposition which they overcame or which defeated them, may be of help as well as of interest in the critical years which lie ahead for all incompleted conservation projects.

TO USE OR TO KEEP?

THE conservation movement took its earliest form seeking control of the natural resources on the nation's public domain, which, in the 1890s, was in the neighborhood of one billion acres. The question was: Should the public lands be stripped of their natural resources for private gain, or should they be wisely cropped under the supervision of the Federal government through long decades on a sustained-yield basis? Much of the area of the public lands was still relatively unknown, despite the fact that hunters and prospectors and ranchers had tramped or ridden over millions of acres. Boundaries were in dispute and surveys were sketchy. Such little control as the Federal government exercised over these areas was casual and ineffective and was carried out by agents, most of whom were political appointees with little knowledge of boundaries and regulations.

Settlers near public lands took it for granted that they were entitled to use the natural resources, whether for grazing, or cutting timber, or for water, and that the principle of "first come first served" was not only fair but practicable. They regarded efforts of the Federal government to restrict such uses as intolerable.

In other words even before the conservation movement began to gain strength in the East (which was not until after the succession of Theodore Roosevelt to the Presidency), conservation was bitterly opposed in the West, where almost all the public lands lay. Westerners resented giving the Federal government the right to restrict the uses of the Federal land, and resisted efforts to establish a corps of trained agents of enforcement to impose Washington-made restrictions on the use of the public domain. If there was to be any kind of "conserving," Westerners were determined that this should be done by the states, whose political leaders were naturally sympathetic to local wishes and prejudices, rather than to the distant and unfriendly Federal government. It was their good fortune that in the East the public was either ignorant of, or apathetic to, the conservation of natural resources and that Republican presidents from Andrew Johnson through William McKinley were not noted for keenness or breadth of vision. Most Republican leaders tended to favor whatever "big business" wanted, and it was clear even in the nineties that influential businessmen throughout the West (often backed by wealthy Easterners) did not wish to see the use of public lands regulated. Many hoped to do on a large scale what small ranchers had done on a small scale—use for their own profit as much of the natural resources on public lands as they could control.

The situation was further complicated by the fact that in the nineties the civil service as we now know it was still in embryo. Most posts in governments of all levels were held by political appointees who knew and cared little about their jobs except for the pay. Furthermore, the Federal government was cumbersome and had grown haphazardly. Gifford Pinchot mentioned in his autobiographical volume, *Breaking New Ground,* that in his first years in Washington there were three separate Federal bureaus that dealt with mineral resources, four or five concerned with streams, half a dozen with authority over forests, and a dozen or so with supervision over wildlife, soils, soil erosion, and other problems of the land. Not only this, but there were such absurdities as that all the forests were under the Department of the Interior but the only two foresters in the government employ were in the Department of Agriculture and had nothing to do with the forests officially. The duties of the political appointees who administered the public lands were prescribed in laws. "Some of these [laws] were good," Pinchot wrote, "but all of them were badly—and more often than not, corruptly—administered." And he prophesied that the forest reserves would bear the scars of Interior Department mismanagement for generations to come, thanks to the domination of what he called "a densely ignorant office" over a "politically chosen field force."

Fortunately a few influential national leaders in the early 1900s saw clearly the dangers of unplanned and uncontrolled exploitation of the nation's natural resources. Two men, in particular, were determined to stop it. One of them, Theodore Roosevelt, is still remembered for his support of conservation. The other, Gifford Pinchot, who was the chief "idea man" of the conservation movement in its early days, was one of the few trained foresters in the United States and was chosen by President Roosevelt to organize the U.S. Forest Service in the Department of Agriculture. Like most men with missions, Pinchot aroused strong reactions. His many friends eagerly followed his leadership. His staff worshipped him. Yet to some of his fellow workers in the field of conservation he seemed arbitrary, opinionated, and devious. Although I was too young to have talked much with him while he was leading the conservation cause, I saw enough of him later to have been beguiled by his charm and his clarity of mind. He was tough and shrewd in attaining his ends, yet gentle and sensitive to beauty. A cultivated cosmopolitan with wide interests, including a thorough knowledge of German and French, he yet was a great outdoors man, hardy, tireless, and fearless, a crack shot and skilled horseman. Today his political philosophy would probably be tagged "left of center," as he favored using government to restrain unscrupulous "rugged individualists." Yet on rereading *Breaking New Ground* I am sure that he was a builder rather than a visionary. He was determined to put an end to the wasting of the nation's natural resources and he worked relentlessly to devise and impose means for their long-range use in the public, rather than in private, interests.

Pinchot's approach was practical. His first goal was to establish order and equity in the handling of the natural resources in the public domain. To him "order" meant honest and efficient administration, in contrast to the shoddy practices which prevailed in the Department of the Interior when he first knew it in the 'nineties. In place of the traditional political appointees, he wanted a corps of trained rangers who knew forestry and who would not be afraid to enforce the regulations of the bureau. To find young men well-fitted for this work was his first major task. Fortunately he had a gift of instilling enthusiasm and high ideals among those who came to work for him.

Pinchot's own account of the methods and the ideals of the

Forest Service as he built it up is illuminating. The service, he explained, had a great purpose and was organized on the principle of individual regulation and responsibility. In setting up a job the bureau first sought the right man and then saw to it that he knew the scope and limits of his task. The next step was to give him his head and let him use it. The chosen man had the chance to do his work, and the means to do it, to the limit of the bureau's power to provide them. Furthermore, he received full credit for the good work which he did. The Forest Service was, as Pinchot explained, "not an organization of master and servant, it was a service of mutual effort for a common purpose. We are all working together towards the same end." Good work was rewarded by promotion, and the morale of the service was strengthened by promoting its own people instead of looking for new blood outside. Most of the young men who joined the service did so because of the urge to do good work in a good cause, rather than because of a desire to earn good money (which, incidentally, the service did not pay). In summing up, Pinchot said that most important of all was the fact that "every member of the Service realized that it was engaged in a great and necessary undertaking in which the whole future of their country was at stake. The Service had a clear understanding of where it was going. It was determined to get there and it was never afraid to fight for what was right."

When the transfer of the forest lands from the Department of the Interior to the Department of Agriculture was completed, the Forest Service issued a manual for its personnel commonly referred to as the "Use Book." According to this manual the timber, water, pasture, mineral, and other resources of the forest reserves were for the use of the people and could be obtained under reasonable conditions without

rves. Often the Administration leaders of the conservation
rces found themselves severely checked, and in one case al-
ost checkmated.

The case dramatizes the determined opposition of Western
ngressmen to the development of policies for the use of
rest lands, and at the same time it points up the shrewdness
th which President Roosevelt circumvented them. The in-
dent grew out of a decision of Congress to deprive the Present of long-held powers to establish National Forests by
esidential proclamation. Western congressmen had had
eir fill of forest reserves and they knew that he wanted
re and more. They also knew that if they tried to curb
m by act of Congress, the President would almost surely
o such a bill, and that they might find it hard to override
e veto. Accordingly, they resorted to the use of a "rider"
ich they attached to the Sundry Civil Bill, which included
propriations for the Department of Agriculture. The pol-
ians believed that the President would not risk vetoing
h an appropriations bill, and that as he could not veto the
er by itself, he would have to approve the appropriations
, and thus be curbed henceforth by the terms of the rider.
n this instance the members of Congress who attached the
er forgot that they were dealing with a shrewd antagonist.
e deadline for signing the bill containing the rider was
days from the date of its transmission to the President—
days during which TR, aided by Pinchot and other mem
of the Forest Service, picked out about 18,000,000 acre
e most desirable portions of the public domain not ye
gnated as National Forests and ordered that these be se
e as such forthwith by presidential proclamation. Then-
not until the seal of the Secretary of State had been a
l to the proclamations establishing the new nation

delay. Legitimate improvements and business enterprises
were to be encouraged. The forest reserves were to be open
to all persons for all lawful purposes. Those who wished to
make a use of the forest reserves for which a permit was required were to consult the nearest forest officer. The "Use
Book" explained that the forest reserves are "for the purpose
of preserving a perpetual supply of timber for home industries, preventing destruction of the forest cover which regu-
lates the flow of streams, and protecting residents from unfair
competition in the use of forest and range." This was an elaboration of Pinchot's early definition of the function of forestry as being: "to make the forests produce the largest possible amount of *whatever crop or service will be most useful,*
and keep on producing for generation after generation of
men and trees." [Italics mine—NR.] Later he enlarged this
concept: "It must be clearly borne in mind that all land is to
be devoted to its most productive use for the permanent good
of the whole people, and not for the temporary benefits of
individuals or companies." He capped this with a phrase
coined by one of his most effective associates, W J McGee,
who defined the new policy as "the use of the natural resources for the greatest good of the greatest number for the
longest time."

From these brief extracts it is clear that the Forest Service
was early giving form to what is now termed "multiple use"—
a misnomer, in fact, for what might more accurately be called
"controlled uses." As I amplify in Chapter VI, multiple use
as practiced in recent decades is predicated on planning and
regulation. The very size of the forest reserves implies that
they contain different kinds of land with soils and climates
best suited for different uses. Chief among the Forest Service's concerns were the protection of watersheds and the

courses of streams, the exercise of fire prevention and suppression, the admission under control of grazing on certain types of land for varying lengths of time, the authorization for the continuing search for, and occasional development of, mineral deposits, and, of course, the regulated harvesting of timber under careful supervision. Homesteading was taken for granted, but no one expected that a substantial population engaged in farming would ever live in any of the National Forests—and none did. Although in these early days hunting and fishing on most of the forest reserves was expected, accepted and regulated, other recreational uses of the forests did not become an important part of the multiple use concept until after World War I, when the development of motoring on a large scale brought forest lands within the reach of increasing millions of vacationists. Only since the 1930s has the establishment and protection of wilderness areas been an important function of the U. S. Forest Service (see Chapter VII). It is pertinent to note that except for these wilderness areas the common denominator in all these Forest Service activities is "use." The use was and is for different purposes, but the implication is clear that the resources on U. S. National Forest lands are for long range consumption.

It is difficult for Easterners to realize the depth of the antagonism of politicians, businessmen, ranchers, chambers of commerce and almost everyone living within an easy reach of National Forests or Parks against the initial setting aside of these reserves and against all efforts to enlarge them or to tighten the regulations governing their use. I have talked with many persons about this in the last fifty years. Opposition rests on a number of postulates. First is the dislike of interference in local affairs by the Federal government. Next, Westerners resent the assumption of many nonresidents that

they have not only a right but a duty to tell
how they should deal with public lands i
hood—which obviously is a way to lose frien
people.

Outsiders also ignore political factors of
Of these the fact that most public lands ar
rolls has long been a major irritant, and th
that some Forest Service lands do provide
of "in lieu" monies to the county treasurie
dents are resentful that these public lands
ably never will be, available for unrestric
development. If they could be exploite
bring at least temporary prosperity to th
is one reason why any suggested enlarger
park—especially if the enlargement is to
the purchase of privately owned lands r
exchange between Federal land-owning
and resented locally. Another problem is
or low-cost grazing on public lands, wh
began as a natural form of appropriatic
word for unauthorized and unpaid use
came to be regarded as a privilege, and
the Federal government, was hotly de
morial right. In other words, the use of
tinues to be intertwined with local ec
interests.

The new chief forester was able in n
come the antagonism of senators and c
political leaders in the West to the deve
forest service to protect the National
But most congressmen continued to a
propriations requested for the mainte

forests—he signed the appropriations bill which carried the rider which put an end to his powers thus to set aside reserves. His enemies in Congress had pulled his political teeth —but not until after he had bitten off a large part of the forest lands which Congress had determined must not be included as national forests. TR's comment on this incident in his Autobiography was that the congressional leaders who had sought to curb him "turned handsprings in their wrath."

Since 1906 the Forest Service has done the work for which TR and Pinchot created it, and is an outstanding example of how the utilitarian functions of conservation can be put into effective use by the Federal Government. The extent to which the Forest Service has kept up with the changing interpretation of the term "conservation" may be judged from the fact that whereas in 1925 the number of visitors to the Forests totaled slightly less than 5,000,000, in 1967 they numbered about 150,000,000. The Forest Service is expecting that the rate of increase of visitors will continue, and perhaps even accelerate, in the years ahead because the ever-growing population near National Forests is becoming increasingly aware of the many fine recreational opportunities in the forest lands.

Younger by a dozen years than the Forest Service, the National Park Service from its start had distinctly different objectives than those of the Forest Service. Its work has been primarily protective, and its goal has been the safeguarding of scenic values for the long-range enjoyment of vacationists and sightseers. The Park Service has consistently opposed the commercial development of natural resources inside National Parks and Monuments. It is interesting to note that even before the present National Park Service was formed, the Department of the Interior in a publication entitled "Glimpses of Our National Parks" (published in 1916) stated: "The national parks, unlike the national forests, are not properties in a commercial sense, but natural preserves for the rest, recreation and education of the people. They remain under nature's own chosen conditions. They alone maintain the 'forest primeval.'" This was further amplified in the first annual report of the director of the National Park Service, which quoted the enabling act that described the purpose of the National Park Service as being "to conserve the scenery and the natural historic objects and the wildlife therein, and to provide for the enjoyment of same in such manner and by such means as *will leave them unimpaired for the enjoyment of future generations.*" [Italics mine—N.R.]

I emphasize these differences in objectives between the park and forest services because I think that they are not understood by many conservationists. Yet they are at the base of the bureaucratic rivalries which still divide these two highly competitive and competent government services. In fairness to both it should be noted that the difference in policies and attitudes stems from their statutory functions. There are as good arguments in favor of excluding commercial operations from National Parks as could be made against imposing on the Forest Service the kind of rigid and excluding controls which the National Park Service has adopted. The forests are for use. The parks are for the preservation of their scenic resources for present and future enjoyment.

What Pinchot was to the newly formed Forest Service, Stephen T. Mather became to the newly formed National Park Service, which he took over in 1917. Mather, like Pinchot, had the capacity for winning and holding the devotion of his assistants. Like Pinchot he was a man of considerable wealth. A graduate of the University of California, Mather spent five years on the *New York Sun* in the days of its famous editor and owner, Charles A. Dana, and then went into business in Chicago and made a substantial fortune. He was a friend of Franklin K. Lane, who served as Secretary of the Interior under Wilson. Like Pinchot, Mather was a great outdoors man and an indefatigable hiker, mountain climber, and camper. His interest in the possibilities of developing the more spectacular parts of the West for recreation purposes was the natural outgrowth of having done much tramping not only in the California Sierra but through most of the few National Parks already in existence in the early 1900s. These parks, when Mather took over, were, to quote Gilbert Grosvenor, publisher of the *National Geographic Magazine,* "poorly managed—without authority, without central appropriations, without sufficient accommodations for visitors, without efficient personnel—without almost everything (except, of course, the natural wonders themselves)." In other words, to Mather fell the task of creating an efficient National Park Service and of helping to acquire additional parks and monuments, and to make them available to a steadily increasing number of visitors. It was largely due to his combination of imagination and generosity that he was able to carry out these tasks. Like Pinchot he was a good picker of assistants, as may be judged from the fact that two of those who were with him from the start, Arno B. Cammerer and Horace M. Albright, became, in turn, director of the National Park Service. Like Pinchot, Mather sought and obtained intense loyalty and devotion from all who worked for him.

My own contacts with Mather were brief, and occurred during the struggle to prevent lumber companies from cutting trees on land which they owned within the boundaries of Yosemite National Park (see Chapter IV). From those who knew him well I learned that his early newspaper training had given him an awareness of the mechanics, as well as the value, of good public relations, and that he deliberately interested influential persons to visit different National Parks, and possible areas to be included in new parks, in the hope that their support could help in attaining desired objectives. He knew that if the National Park Service was to prosper it must have widespread public backing for its program.

Of his assistants none played a more important role than Horace M. Albright, who, although years younger than Mather, early became Mather's "alter ego." Albright, with whom I have had many associations since Mather's death in 1930, still speaks of Mather with a combination of respect and affection. His belief that Mather belongs among the great figures in the conservation movement is based on close observation and knowledge. This estimate carries special weight because it comes from a man whose own contributions to conservation in America are unequaled. For the last half century Albright has consistently been constructive in his approach and generous in his support of others working in conservation fields. His years of experience in dealing with politicians have made him fully aware of the fact that without the support of key leaders in both houses of Congress no government bureau or department can function effectively. At the same time he has repeatedly given others the benefit of his long experience and sound judgment. I owe to him not only much of my understanding of the conservation movement in the last half century, but also useful lessons in the effective mobilization of public opinion in behalf of worthwhile projects.

The National Park Service celebrated its fiftieth anniversary in 1966. The U. S. Forest Service is only eleven years older. It is largely due to the work of these two bureaus that conservation objectives were first attained on public lands, and that the conservation movement throughout the country got off the ground. Each bureau went its own way with its own ideals and prescribed goals. Today they control most of the Federally owned lands devoted to conservation. The Bureau of Land Management in the Department of the Interior administers even larger areas of public lands, but most of these have relatively restricted conservation potentials. The Department of Defense has substantial holdings of public lands, but it is unlikely that these will be available for other than military uses. In addition, numerous states have developed good state park systems, and some have also set aside forest lands as state reserves. Their role is likely to increase in the decades ahead.

Outside of government there are, of course, long-established organizations of private citizens which have made major contributions to the cause of conservation. Their number is now so great that merely to list them would fill pages. Some among them have rendered great services in the field of education. One in particular, the Save-the-Redwoods League, has continued through the last fifty years to render great educational service and to further the acquisition of valuable groves of the finest redwoods (see Chapter XVI).

3

PARADISE LOST

THIRTY years before Gifford Pinchot developed the U. S. Forest Service and a full forty years before Stephen T. Mather organized the National Park Service, a long-legged, lean, bearded Scot, who had been brought to the United States as a boy, fell in love with the Yosemite Valley in California. Year after year he returned and from the Yosemite explored the California Sierra, studying marks of glaciation, mapping streams, listing flowers, viewing the occasional groves of *sequoia gigantea*—the "big trees"—with a mixture of awe and pride. This was John Muir, who between 1869 and 1914 tramped over every trail—and off many of them—in the Sierra from south to north.

A friend and occasional camping companion of his, Joseph LeConte, professor of geology at the University of California in Berkeley, wrote of Muir in his journal on one of these trips: "Mr. Muir gazes and gazes and cannot get his fill. He is a most passionate lover of nature. Plants and flowers and forests and skies and clouds and mountains seem actually to haunt his imagination. . . . He is really not only an intelligent man, as I saw at once, but a man of strong, earnest nature, and of a thoughtful, closely observing, original mind."

Muir combined the reasoning processes of a scientist with the soul of a poet. At the same time that he gloried in the spectacles of nature that he saw on his hikes through the Sierra, Muir made precise notes of the work of glaciers and meticulously recorded details—the effect of winds on waterfalls, the melting of snow on evergreens, the sudden appearance and evaporation of clouds, and countless interrelationships of a kind usually overlooked by specialists. Long before the word "ecology" became part of the patter of naturalists, Muir noted that if one layer of nature was disturbed in a given area, the effect was transmitted in that area to others, often with far-reaching consequences. If lumbermen logged the upper reaches of a watershed, its soils would be washed miles downstream, helping cause floods which could—and often did—gouge out and destroy forests that had stood unscathed for centuries. Overgrazing led to erosion, which, in turn, could lower the water table and dry up streams.

To this clear sight he added the gift of plain speech, with the result that what he wrote was sought by editors and widely read for years. These writings stressed the need to save fine bits of America's scenic heritage. In time Muir became the chief spokesman for conservation in the country. In California, where so many of the finest of the nation's scenic resources are grouped, he was early hailed as a prophet and had many followers. He helped found the Sierra Club in San Francisco in 1892 and was its first president, which office he held until his death in 1914. The relationship was made to order. Muir knew the Sierra better than any of his associates. Its preservation was close to his heart. Thanks to the wide appeal of his writings, it was easy for him to spread his views throughout the country.

While Muir and Pinchot had traits in common—each was an idealist, and each was devoted to the "great outdoors"— the differences in their philosophies of conservation were basic. To Pinchot conservation was a political means for achieving a utilitarian end. Muir looked on conservation as a practical way to preserve beauty—a concept which relatively few then grasped. I am sure that as a Calvinist, Muir often must have thought of the words of the Psalmist: "Eyes have they but they see not. They have ears but they hear not." Yet to him the truth was clear. He had seen it in the big trees, in the carpets of wildflowers, in the waterfalls and granite domes of Yosemite that had weathered a million storms, in the burgeoning thunderheads that rose up from behind the ranges, piling gray and brown shadows beneath their sun-blazened tops.

These things he knew. They meant much to him. Any fool could dam a canyon or cut a big tree. Only God—or call it nature, if you will—could make the waterfalls in the Yosemite, and these took aeons in the making. Where Pinchot thought in decades, Muir thought in millennia. Pinchot's concept of use was that of a prudent steward, and the nation owes him thanks for his fight to save natural resources for long-range consumption. But Muir's eyes were on spiritual, not on material, values—on the everlasting rather than the transient. The ultimate use that utilitarians preached seemed to him not only misuse but desecration. He wished to save for all time—not just for the brief span before demand became consumption.

It was Muir's good fortune that the Sierra Club in 1900 chose as its secretary a young man from San Francisco by the name of William E. Colby, who was to hold that office for forty-four years and then become the Club's president. The two worked well together. Muir was the dreamer, Colby the doer. Muir preached a holy war. Colby recruited the crusaders. Colby was a giant of a man, physically powerful, courageous, and tenacious, with a clear mind. He shared Muir's love of the Sierra, and of sequoias and the foothills covered with flowers. Where Muir was the prophet crying in the wilderness, Colby transmuted Muir's vision into a powerful weapon in behalf of conservation causes.

Muir died before my first trip to California, which was early in 1928. I met Colby that year after my visit to Yosemite, and corresponded with him thenceforth until both of us moved to Big Sur, where, for the last eighteen years of his life, we were neighbors and friends and worked together on conservation projects. He died at the age of eighty-nine, vigorous, vital, and alert until the end—a truly rugged individualist who matched in form and almost in appearance the Sierra that he and Muir so dearly loved. Where Muir liked to hike and climb by himself, Colby for years led groups of young Sierra Club members over tough trails, and despite his huge frame, could outwalk and outclimb men and women many years his junior.

Colby had admiration, respect, and affection for Muir. He appreciated Muir's sense of values and relied on his thorough knowledge of the Sierra range. Colby told me that no one had hiked and climbed in the Sierra as extensively as had John Muir. Surely no one knew better the damage caused by cattle ranchers, sheepherders, lumbermen, and miners. Muir had walked over miles of barren ground, stripped of almost every blade of grass by sheep and cattle—"hoofed locusts," he called them. He had seen the desecration caused by mines, whether abandoned or in operation. He had grieved at the waste and brutal destructiveness of the loggers.

Just as Colby respected Muir, so Muir had faith in the young secretary's hardheadedness and effectiveness in winning friends for conservation among influential Californians. Colby knew how to turn people toward good causes. A lawyer by training—he became one of the leading authorities on mining law and water rights—he was skilled in drafting briefs and statements and in compiling brochures. Lucid, frank, and fearless he was also shrewd and farseeing. Those who worked with him knew that he could be a rough foe. He was a big man in all senses of the word—in reasoning powers, and as a leader in good causes. Having often seen him in action I am glad that I was on his side rather than against him.

It is interesting that this essentially practical, efficient, and hardheaded lawyer should have strongly sensed the spiritual quality in Muir. In a letter which Colby wrote only a few weeks before his death he said that Muir believed that "nature was an expression of the divine spirit. He saw the spirit shining forth wherever he turned." Colby added that Muir's "later writings were essentially spiritual in character, and in his life he became a living expression of this spirituality."

What was in many ways the climax of the continuing collaboration between Muir and Colby was their fight against the plans of the city of San Francisco to dam and flood Hetch Hetchy Valley in Yosemite National Park and make it San Francisco's main source of water and of electric power. Muir, who knew every part of Hetch Hetchy, described that valley as "a counterpart of Yosemite and one of the most sublime and beautiful and important features of the park. . . . Its falls and groves and delightful backgrounds are surpassed or equaled only in the Yosemite. These sacred mountain tem-

ples are the holiest ground that the heart of man has conse-
crated, and it behooves us all faithfully to do our part in see-
ing that our wild mountain parks are passed on unspoiled to
those who come after us, for they are national properties to
which every man has a right and interest." It is pertinent that
J. D. Whitney, the famous geologist after whom Mount Whitney was named, wrote in 1868 that Hetch Hetchy was "almost
an exact counterpart of the Yosemite," and added: "it is not
on quite as grand a scale as that valley, but if there were no
Yosemite the Hetch Hetchy would be fairly entitled to a
world-wide fame."

The controversy that brought this strange name to nation-
wide attention began in the early 1900s. The project of damming Hetch Hetchy had much support in San Francisco because it was well known that the existing sources of water
which the city was using were becoming less adequate as
population increased. To dam Hetch Hetchy, remote as it
was from San Francisco, did not present insurmountable engineering problems. The site itself was described by one of
its proponents in hyperbolic terms: "There is not on this
round earth in all probability so fine a site prepared by nature for a reservoir from which to supply human beings with
some of the principal requisites of life."

At the first mention of the damming of Hetch Hetchy the
conservationists, spearheaded by Muir and Colby, were up
in arms. Their arguments against the project were threefold:

(1) The Hetch Hetchy Valley was one of the most spectacular valleys in the entire Sierra, surpassed in magnificence
only by Yosemite itself. It should be saved, not flooded.

(2) As Hetch Hetchy was an important segment of the
Yosemite National Park its use as a dam and power site would

set a precedent for other commercial invasions of Yosemite and other national parks.

(3) As Hetch Hetchy was not the only potential source of water and hydroelectric power for the Bay Area, there was no compelling reason to flood this particular valley, which belonged to the nation as a whole, for the exclusive benefit of the city of San Francisco.

In considering these objections the city authorities took the conventional position that their duty to the municipality was clear and simple: to get the best possible supply of water at the cheapest cost to the citizens. They denied that they had any responsibility about what might happen to scenic values in remote parts of the Sierra which were practically never visited by San Franciscans and had probably not even been heard of by more than a fraction of 1 per cent of the people of California. Most of them knew little about conservation, and cared less. Faced with a choice between being able to supply their constituents with plenty of good water at a fair price or of refusing to tap a desirable source because it was proclaimed by a group of nonresident nature-lovers to be particularly beautiful, they took the water and let the beauty go. They did exactly as nine hundred and ninety-nine out of a thousand other local boards would have done—they looked after the interests of their own people first.

The argument that it was wrong for a city to invade a National Park for a supply of water carried little weight in those days. The National Park Service was not even in existence when Hetch Hetchy was turned over to San Francisco. There were no rigid standards of use for national park lands, such as were developed and adhered to in the last half century. In other words, the idea that no part of a national park was ever to be used for any nonpark commercial purpose was still in a

dim future. It is true that members of the Sierra Club stressed
the importance of the sanctity of national park lands, but they
were far ahead of national policy.

As for the third point—the suggestion that there were
other sites from which San Francisco could get water besides
Hetch Hetchy Valley—a rereading of some of the accounts of
the struggle suggests that from a technical point of view such
sources existed but that probably they would have cost more
than would Hetch Hetchy.

In the Sierra Club the Hetch Hetchy fight became a major
issue. Muir and Colby, supported by a substantial majority
of the club membership, fought vigorously in defense of saving the valley. But it is interesting to note that in the club
membership at this time was also one of the leaders supporting the city's position—Warren Olney, Sr., in whose office
the by-laws of the club had been drawn up in 1892, and who
served as its vice-president when it was incorporated. Olney
was a distinguished lawyer and became mayor of Oakland.
His grandson, Warren Olney, III, who was Assistant Attorney
General of the United States under President Eisenhower,
and then was appointed administrator of the Federal Judici-
ary, gave me xeroxed copies of two articles which the elder
Olney wrote which set forth in detail the reasons why Hetch
Hetchy was the perfect site for the city's source of water. Olney wrote as a partisan—just as did Muir and Colby—but the
cause as he presented it is worth special consideration today
because when contrasted with the attitude of the conservationists it dramatizes the basic split which seems to be inherent in almost all problems connected with conservation—the
split between the *users* and the *savers* to which I have already
referred.

Olney's argument started from the premise that the cities

in the Bay Area should own their own water supply, and that the existing sources of water which were in the hands of private corporations would soon be inadequate for the cities' needs. "They must purchase, and desire and intend to purchase," he wrote, "the local water plants and water resources, but to meet the needs of the increasing population and the growing needs of civilization more water must be obtained from a distance." He went on to explain that plenty of water could only be had from a few streams on the western slopes of the Sierra. Of these the only one from which it might be got at a fair rate was the Tuolumne River, which had its source in Yosemite National Park. Mr. Olney summarized the advantages of this river by saying: "It has the largest watershed, and the best watershed, and it has a larger flow and far and away a better reservoir site, [Hetch Hetchy] than any of the other streams accessible to the people."

He then brought up a legal argument based on the existence of privately owned lands inside the park which had been patented before the park boundaries had been established. There is relevance in what he says about this to national parks today, Yosemite included, where the problem of inholdings—parcels of privately held land inside of the park boundaries—is still troublesome.

The way Olney put it is that "the United States government many years ago parted with its title to the larger part of the floor of Hetch Hetchy Valley to certain individuals. After the land had been patented to these people the City of San Francisco bought these lands. What was desired of the United States government was that the United States should consent to the flooding of these lands in the valley to which the United States retains title. That is to say that if a dam is built at the lower end of the valley and the land flooded by an artificial lake, the lake will cover land belonging to the City of San Francisco, and also lands belonging to the United States. What was wanted was an act of Congress authorizing an exchange of the lands belonging to the United States on the floor of the valley for lands outside of the valley owned by the city." Mr. Olney then added a sentence that expresses a point of view which, if sustained by the courts, could undermine the whole system and negate the purpose of national parks: *"The City of San Francisco can do whatever it pleases with its own land in the Hetch Hetchy Valley.* [Italics mine— N.R.] It wants the other lands on the floor of the valley so that there can be no objection to turning this valley into a lake." This point of view can be a threat to the integrity of any national park, for the obvious reason that so long as there are lands within the border of national parks owned either by private individuals or by government units other than the National Park Service, the mere existence of these inholdings can interfere with many conservation objectives.

Mr. Olney then described the excellence of the Hetch Hetchy Valley as a dam site. He said that a dam two hundred and fifty feet high could be constructed at comparatively small expense, and that as the floor of the valley is level, an immense quantity of water could be impounded.

The details of the struggle to save the Hetch Hetchy Valley are now of interest only to historians. There is little to be gained by considering the "might-have-beens." After long delays Congress acted, and in December, 1913 President Wilson signed the bill empowering San Francisco to take over Hetch Hetchy. The dam as originally planned was completed in 1923, and in 1938 was raised to the present height of more than three hundred feet.

The argument had dragged on for years. The Sierra Club,

ably aided by J. Horace McFarland of the American Civic Association and Robert Underwood Johnson, editor of the *Century Magazine,* and other Eastern advocates of conservation, argued before congressional committees. Feelings ran high—especially when it became known that Gifford Pinchot sided with the city of San Francisco on the strictly utilitarian ground that the greatest good for the greatest number would be better served by furnishing good water to San Francisco's hundreds of thousands of citizens than by saving Hetch Hetchy Valley for a few hundred tourists a year to enjoy. Some of the contestants still speak bitterly of Pinchot as if he had betrayed his principles, whereas the truth is that he had not progressed as far toward the concept of the preservation of scenic beauty as had his critics. James R. Garfield, who had been Secretary of the Interior under Theodore Roosevelt, was also bitterly attacked as having "sold out" the National Parks by agreeing to the turning over of this fine corner of Yosemite National Park for commercial exploitation. In fairness to Garfield two things should be pointed out. The first is that his approval of Hetch Hetchy was made with the distinct reservation that the area in the neighborhood of Lake Eleanor, also in the Hetch Hetchy drainage, should be tapped and used before anything was done to Hetch Hetchy. The second is that in those early days—the winter of 1912–13—the concept of the territorial inviolability of a national park to which I have already referred had received little thoughtful consideration. In retrospect there can be no doubt that the damming of Hetch Hetchy was an unjustifiable use of national park land. But this use was granted three years before the National Park Service came into existence.

The conservationists lost the battle of Hetch Hetchy. San Francisco dammed the Valley. Muir was crushed and aging rapidly. He died in the following year, unaware that although the battle had been lost the cause of conservation had gained many recruits. Muir had pointed the way which others would follow. It was an early and striking example of the fact that the impetus in nearly all conservation projects comes not from political leaders or even from bureaucrats, but rather from determined and dedicated private citizens. Despite their failure, Muir, Colby, and the Sierra Club had given heart to other conservationists fighting for other cherished goals. Few conservation causes are forever won, whereas many can be forever lost—as was Hetch Hetchy. Conservation calls for eternal vigilance. Government can neither lead nor save. It can only administer and occasionally stave off—and then only if public opinion is loud and clear and united.

In their day Muir and Colby and others who opposed the damming of Hetch Hetchy were denounced as mere visionaries and enemies of progress, which in the America of the early 1900s were words of scorn and contempt. Yet time, the healer, while it cannot repair the harm done by damming Hetch Hetchy, can at least help to put causes in perspective. Nothing better illustrates this then does a paper prepared only a few years ago by the daughter of one of the chief sponsors of the city's plans for damming Hetch Hetchy, Warren Olney the elder. Writing about her father's part in the controversy and stressing his concern about the importance of substituting municipal ownership of water for the private ownership that had persisted down into the twentieth century, she went on to express the opinion that her father at the time felt that as the protection of the Yosemite itself was assured, a compromise about Hetch Hetchy was in order. To which she appended the clear-sighted comment that: "He did not foresee the day when the Sierra would be so crowded, and unspoiled natural grandeur in such short supply, that Hetch Hetchy Valley would loom in retrospect as a bit of Paradise lost." From what I have heard of Olney, Sr., I think that if he could judge the case in the light of what we now know and can see, he would concur with his daughter's view. He won his fight, unaware that San Francisco's victory would be the nation's loss.

4

TRADING LAND FOR TREES

FIFTEEN years after the Hetch Hetchy defeat in the Yosemite, a combination of lucky breaks enabled the National Park Service to avoid turning over valuable tracts of exceptionally fine sugar pines in Yosemite National Park to one of the big lumber companies. In the process a useful precedent was established for acquiring a portion, at least, of land inside national parks legally owned by individuals or organizations.

Chance placed me in a good position to lend a hand. My first visit to Yosemite was in February 1928. When I had been there a few days the park superintendent asked me if I would like to go with two of the park rangers on a snowshoeing trip into the high Sierra to measure the accumulated snowfall—a routine job which the rangers performed every two weeks to record the total annual precipitation. I enjoyed snowshoeing and was glad thus to be able to see parts of the park which were closed to visitors in winter. We packed food and warm clothing and were to sleep in a ranger cabin where blankets and firewood were stored against such visits. Before dawn the next morning we left the floor of the valley and climbed into the mountains as the sunrise silhouetted the crest of the Sierra east of us.

During the two days of our trip the rangers, John Wegner and Bill Merrill, talked freely about the problems of the park and mentioned that the Park Service was about to turn over to one of the lumber companies a large area of sugar pines just inside the western boundary of the park in exchange for tracts which the lumber company owned near the center of the park—tracts which the Park Service needed and which were scheduled soon to be stripped of their timber by the owners.

This was my first contact with problems of "inholdings," which still plague the National Park Service. I had taken for granted that all the land within the borders of a national park was government owned, but the rangers explained that these so-called "inholdings" inside national parks had the same legal status as homesteaded or otherwise legally acquired land outside the boundaries of a park. The Federal government has no jurisdiction over them even though they are within the boundaries of a national preserve.

The more we talked about the planned trade, the more outrageous it struck me. When I insisted that this sort of thing should not be allowed, the rangers replied that perhaps I was right, but that it was being done at that very moment. As I continued to protest, they suggested that I talk with the park superintendent when we returned to the valley.

This I did. He told me that the decision had been made in Washington and that he could do nothing to protest it. He suggested that I talk with the director of the National Park Service, Mr. Mather, who, with his chief assistant, Horace M. Albright, was due in Yosemite the following day to attend the annual conference of the superintendents of all the national parks.

When I got back to the hotel, I called Albright, who was an old friend. He had just checked in, and when I told him how I felt about the deal with the lumber company he suggested that I join him for supper and said that he would brief me about it. When we met he repeated what the rangers had said—that the Park Service had no money to buy these tracts and that Congress had no inclination to appropriate funds for this purpose. This meant that the only way in which the Park Service could acquire the property that it wanted to protect was by a trade. After long negotiations with the lumber company it was agreed that the Park Service would grant those lands with fine stands of sugar pines just inside the western boundary of the park where tourists rarely visited, in exchange for the lumber company's holdings near the center of the park, which the Park Service was particularly anxious to control because they were scheduled soon to be logged. The sugar-pine lands would be eliminated from the park's total area, but thanks to the trade the Park Service would reduce substantially the total acreage of privately owned lands inside the park boundaries. This was good. But the trade also would reduce the overall size of the park, which was regrettable. Albright explained to me that the existence of privately owned lands inside national parks was unavoidable, because when the boundaries of each park were originally drawn it was virtually certain that parcels of privately owned lands would be found within the enclosed areas—parcels which had been legally acquired before the park had been established. The mere fact that a tract of private land became engulfed by park lands in no way curtailed the owner's title to his property. Albright repeated that Congress to date had declined to appropriate funds to buy inholdings in parks.

When I asked him if Mr. Mather might give me an interview for *The New York Times,* he said that he would arrange it. I queried the *Times,* with which I was then associated as an editorial writer, summarizing the situation and asking the managing editor if he wished such an interview. He wired "Yes," and shortly thereafter I talked with Mather.

The director was distressed when I asked him about the trade of park lands for privately owned lands, and repeated what Albright had said, that he had no alternative, as it would cost millions of dollars to buy the land and that the chances that Congress would appropriate money to do so were small.

At this point I said that I questioned his premise that he had no alternative. I suggested that instead of regarding congressional inaction as inevitable he make a statement that *unless Congress would vote money to enable the Park Service to purchase the land owned by the lumber company inside the park,* he would have no choice but to complete the proposed trade with the lumber company. I told him that I was sure that such a statement from him would arouse nationwide interest and support, and explained that I based my reasoning on the simple assumption that if I, who had long been following problems of conservation and the national parks, had not known that such a situation could arise, the chances were great that the country at large knew nothing about it, and that the public would be just as mad as I was. I added that the *Times* would be glad to print a statement from him if he cared to make one.

Mr. Mather hesitated. So I suggested that I draft the kind of interview which I thought might be effective and bring it to him for his consideration. He agreed, and when I gave him

my draft he made some changes and okayed it and I wired it
to the *Times*. It was printed the next morning, February 25,
1928.

The first paragraph, summarizing the story, reads as follows: "Only prompt action by the nation through Congress
or through private enterprise can save the forest lands in
Yosemite Park now privately owned from being stripped, according to a statement today by Stephen T. Mather, Director
of the National Park Service. At present nearly 11,000 acres
of private lands within the Yosemite boundaries are mostly
owned by lumber companies. On these lands are some of the
finest timber in the park, and the Park Service is unable to
protect them from destruction."

Mr. Mather is quoted as saying: "Repeated efforts in the
past have failed to arouse the nation to the fact that these
privately owned lands within the national parks cannot be
preserved by the National Park Service. Unless those remaining are acquired by the Federal government through purchase, or as in the case of the new Appalachian Park, by joint
action with the states, nothing can save them from being denuded of their last sticks of timber."

Under the terms of the proposed exchange of lands with
the lumber company, Mr. Mather pointed out that the suggested trade would reduce by 7,000 acres the total acreage of
privately owned land inside the park boundaries. It would
also involve rectification of these boundaries so that the lands
which the lumber companies were to receive would be cut
out of the park.

"Much as we should hate to see the park area reduced,"
Mr. Mather explained, "we believe it worse for the park that
private lands well within the borders be stripped of trees instead of acquired in exchange for outlying government tim-

ber which could be cut under U. S. Forest Service supervision. They are doomed lands unless private owners can be
enjoined from cutting." He went on to explain that "the Park
Service is powerless to check this destruction. Private owners
are legally empowered to do with the land as they wish. The
only possible remedy is to buy them from the private owners
—a process that is costly and difficult. . . ."

Asked if there was any alternative to curtailing the park
boundary, Mr. Mather replied: "The ideal solution would
be to enlarge the park by acquiring the sugar pine forests
along the border north of the Merced and Tuolumne groves
of giant trees, and by purchasing the privately owned lands in
this area. This would involve even greater expense as about
sixty percent of this land is now privately owned and would
have to be bought from lumber companies." He then re-
verted to the lands inside the park and said: "To acquire
these lands is our first problem. Unless this is done we are
powerless to prevent further destruction of timber within
the park. Already some of the finest forests within the park
boundary have thus been cut. The destruction of the scenic
beauties will continue unless the nation makes a protest so
effective that we can end once and for all the danger of private holdings within the parks being commercially utilized."

A week later *The New York Times* ran on the front page,
on a Sunday, a signed article of mine giving in full the background of the complex situation in the Yosemite which had
led to the crisis. This dispatch was based on long talks with
Albright and the superintendent of Yosemite National Park,
and made detailed references to previous boundary changes
in the history of the Yosemite National Park. It pointed out
that in 1905 there were about 60,000 acres of privately owned
lands within the park boundaries and stated: "As there was

no provision to acquire them it was thought best to eliminate as large a proportion of them as possible from the park. This was done by cutting out a total of about 275,000 acres of land, of which only about 22,500 acres were privately owned. Why it was considered necessary to eliminate from the park ten acres of public land for every acre of privately owned land is one of the mysteries of the Yosemite." The article explained that the next year another boundary change was made, leaving within the park a total of only 19,800 acres of private land. Since that time, by exchanges between the government and private holders, this area was greatly reduced.

The article continued: "The present dangers to the Yosemite are twofold—the boundary change, which will eliminate from the park a large tract of superb uncut forest, and the menace of the remaining privately owned lands within the park, which the owners may despoil as they see fit." I pointed out that the boundary menace was for the time being in abeyance, and then stated: "The menace to the park by the owners of the privately held lands is at the root of the whole trouble. If the private holdings within the park boundaries are acquired by the government there will be no need for any boundary rectification. Until these are acquired they may be cut, or sold for real estate development purposes, or made into amusement parks, or lined with hideous hot-dog stands. Unless they are acquired they are doomed lands. Nothing can be done to save them." I then pointed out that Director Mather had been criticized for not having sooner appealed to the public for help. The dispatch reads: "His failure earlier to adopt an aggressive attitude and, instead of acquiescing in the proposed boundary reduction, to press vigorously for enlargement of the park, and for the acquisition by the Federal government of private holdings within the areas concerned, has delayed, rather than hastened, a solution. Now, however, he is committed to a policy of doing what he can to focus public attention on the necessity of acquiring the privately owned lands within the park.

"Mr. Mather takes the stand that all emphasis should be directed towards this objective. This is the logical view for, if the lands are acquired, the boundary change will not be necessary. Furthermore, if the question of privately owned lands can once be settled one of the gravest dangers to all the parks will be removed." The article concluded by pointing out that there was only one sure solution—to acquire these lands for the government. "To do this there appear to be but three ways: Outright purchase by the Federal government; condemnation and purchase by the State of California with a subsequent transfer of the lands to the Federal government; purchase of the lands by private funds and their transfer to the Federal government."

The reaction to Mather's statement was immediate. Newspapers all over the country urged that Congress appropriate the money to buy up the privately owned lands in the Yosemite, but this was only a start. Editorial opinion had to be translated into political action. Here Albright led the way. He started out by explaining to me that although *The New York Times* had rendered a great service in publicizing the situation, his experience had been that members of Congress cared little for what a metropolitan newspaper said unless they themselves came from the district in which the newspaper was published. He interjected that this, however, was not necessarily the attitude of local newspaper editors, who, as a rule, were glad to reprint comments about problems in their own states, especially if these came from newspapers as well known as *The New York Times*. The congressmen's main concern was what the editors in their own districts wrote. Then Albright asked me—somewhat irrelevantly, I thought—what I planned to do in the next ten days. I said that I was going to Sequoia National Park, and then to Saratoga and Palo Alto, and ultimately to the Monterey peninsula.

"Would you have time to drive down the Valley?" he asked. (For the benefit of those who do not know California, "the Valley" means the great interior valley which is the heartland of California agriculture.)

I asked him what he had in mind.

"If I give you the names of several newspaper men in the Valley," he said, "would you call on them and tell them about our problems here? I ask this because they are the men who will decide what Congress will do in this matter. If you can interest the editors in such California cities as Fresno, Visalia, and Bakersfield they will win over their Congressmen. Without the support of the Congressmen from this part of the state this project will get nowhere. The reason for this is that Congressmen from other districts and states will do nothing unless the local representatives support such a project." He added that the local editors would be glad to see me and would probably ask me to meet with groups of local leaders, and he ended by saying: "If you can show them that you have a sound case we'll have a good chance of winning the battle in Congress."

I told him, of course, that I would do as he suggested. I had a pleasant and interesting time in my brief career as itinerant salesman for the Park Service. Most of the editors were noncommittal, but they were impressed by the fact that *The New York Times* felt that the matter was of sufficient national importance to run several stories and editorials about it.

Albright, who became director of the National Park Service shortly after his return to Washington, saw friends in Congress, including, of course, the representatives from this part of California. Thanks to his tact and persistence he had a friendly reception from the House committee which would hold hearings on the necessary appropriations.

In the meantime a helping hand was extended by Mr. John D. Rockefeller, Jr. According to Mr. Rockefeller's biographer, Mr. Raymond B. Fosdick, Mr. Rockefeller one day "happened upon an editorial in *The New York Times* by Nicholas Roosevelt. Roosevelt had recently visited Yosemite and his editorial conveyed something of his own feeling of shocked horror at the destruction wraught by the logging interests in this area. JDR Jr immediately communicated with the Park Service, asking whether he might be of help. The Park Service was only too ready to offer concrete suggestions, and within a short time Mr. Rockefeller had agreed to put up half the amount needed to preserve the pine forest for the park—an area involving some 15,000 acres. Congress was persuaded to authorize the Secretary of the Interior to match dollar for dollar any amount that could be raised from private sources. Thus with a gift of over one and a half million dollars from JDR Jr and a matching amount from the government, the valuable sugar pines were saved and the scenic approach to Yosemite Valley was secured against future devastation."

Albright brought the project to a successful conclusion. The bulk of the privately owned lands within the boundaries of Yosemite National Park were acquired by purchase. Pertinent to the theme of this book is the fact that the impetus had come from a combination of unrelated coincidences in which by chance a private citizen played the role of catalyst.

I mention this not to claim credit for my small part in the affair, but rather to suggest that in this, as in so many achievements in the field of conservation, a timely "assist" from private citizens helped bring success within reach of the professionals. The transaction was completed rather rapidly—in a little less than two years, which, considering that it involved hearings before committees and the passage of legislation by both houses of Congress, is surprising. One of the obvious reasons for such prompt action is that Representative Louis C. Cramton, who was chairman of the House committee which held the hearings, had for years been an ardent champion of the Park Service and was keenly aware of the need of getting rid of all private land holdings within parks.

When the transaction was concluded Congressman Cramton read into the *Congressional Record* the following letter from Mr. Rockefeller to the Secretary of the Interior, Dr. Ray Lyman Wilbur:

> I enclose herewith a cashier's check made out to your order for $1,709,237.88 on the understanding that the contribution will enable the government to purchase the proposed tract, some 11,000 acres of sugar pine timberland, and add it to Yosemite National Park.
>
> May I take advantage of this opportunity to tell you how highly I esteem the National Park System. I have been in and out of the National Parks and have found that those in charge of them are active and conscientious in serving the interests of the public and making the beauties of the parks available.

Looking back in the light of current costs of lands for parks and recreation, it might be said of Mr. Rockefeller's check for $1,709,237.88 that the land which it helped to buy was cheap at the price. Although the acreage of privately owned lands inside the borders of national parks has been cut since 1928, complete elimination has not yet been achieved. In the Yosemite there are still 2,442 acres in private hands. In Sequoia National Park there are 1,290 acres, mostly concentrated in a small group of summer homes built long before the area was set aside as a national park and owned for the most part by residents of the California valley. Yellowstone still has 2,036 acres of privately owned lands, which, while large in itself, is a fraction of 1 per cent of that park's 2,221,772 acres. In other parks and monuments there are also substantial private holdings, but most of the strategically desirable plots have been acquired and it is now recognized procedure for the Federal government to buy such lands inside national parks and monuments when the need to do so seems to be imperative.

5

CATTLE VERSUS VISITORS

THE preservation of the Teton Mountains in Wyoming and the adjacent Jackson Hole area from which these mountains can best be seen aroused more bitterness and took more time than did the establishment of any other of the National Parks.

The story has lessons for conservationists, and it is with the battle about giving the area park status, rather than with the scenic value of the site, that I shall deal, its value to the public having been confirmed by the fact that in 1966 Grand Teton National Park had more visitors than any other park in the Rocky Mountain states, including Yellowstone and the Grand Canyon.

For the benefit of those who do not know the area it should be pointed out that the northern boundary of the Grand Teton National Park is only six miles south of the southern boundary of Yellowstone National Park. The area known as Jackson Hole would probably, anywhere else in the old West, have been called "Jackson Valley." Its center is a small town called Jackson, which took its name from an early trapper.

The section finally incorporated in the Grand Teton National Park lies north of the town of Jackson. It should also be noted that the Grand Teton National Park in its present form was a piecemeal creation.

The first step was the establishment by act of Congress in 1929 of what is now the northern section of the present Grand Teton National Park, accompanied by the withdrawal of government lands from entry in a large part of the northern portion of the Jackson Hole area, which meant that these lands could not be homesteaded or otherwise acquired by private citizens. In 1930 the United States Senate special wildlife committee visited Jackson Hole and was favorably impressed by the recommendations of a group of local citizens for the addition to the Grand Teton National Park of a larger part of the Jackson Hole area than finally was incorporated into the park. In 1934 the Senate passed a bill introduced by Senator Carey of Wyoming to add the northern part of the Jackson Hole area to the Grand Teton National Park. This bill was approved by the House Public Lands Committee and reported favorably to the House on the last day of that year's session, but was not acted upon before Congress adjourned, and so died.

In 1943 President Franklin D. Roosevelt established the Jackson Hole National Monument by presidential proclamation, following the example of his predecessors who on numerous occasions had created National Monuments by presidential proclamation.

The difference between a national park and a national monument is that an act of Congress is required to establish a national park whereas a national monument is established by a presidential proclamation. Both types of areas are administered by the National Park Service. To date more than eighty National Monuments have been established. Some of these are large, like Death Valley in California; others are small. Some National Parks are small, like Acadia; others like the Great Smokies, or Yellowstone, are relatively large. The purpose of monuments, as of parks, is to give permanent protection to areas of special interest or scenic beauty. But in this case the opposition of the Wyoming politicians was so strong that a bill was passed by both houses of Congress in 1943 to abolish the Jackson Hole National Monument which President Roosevelt had proclaimed. But the President vetoed it, and it was not repassed over his veto. Since then the right of the President to create a national monument has been affirmed by the Supreme Court of the United States.

FDR's proclamation of 1943 creating the Jackson Hole National Monument enraged Wyoming's members of Congress, who contended that the President had resorted to the device of making the Jackson Hole area a national monument as a sly move toward ultimately adding it to the Grand Teton National Park. In retrospect it seems likely that this was what the Executive had in mind. The apparent implication was that because Congress had expressly declined to approve such a move the President had no business to create a national monument out of this particular area. Those who remember FDR's political shrewdness are probably correct in suspecting that the resentment of the Wyoming politicians was as much due to FDR's adroitness in outplaying his adversaries in Congress as it was due to their indignation at his using such a device to circumvent congressional opposition. To him the creation of the Jackson Hole National Monument seemed a smart move in a game he had long been playing with Congress—and winning. The fact that in the process he furthered a good cause added zest to his achievement. In 1950 Jackson

Hole National Monument was incorporated into the Grand Teton National Park in spite of continuing efforts of Wyoming politicians to block it.

Local opposition to this National Monument and to its ultimate inclusion in the Grand Teton National Park was strong and rested on a number of facts, and on assumptions, some of which were mistaken. Among the facts was that the addition of this region to the already large Federal land holdings in Teton County would mean that the Federal government would control 98 per cent of Teton's total area. No wonder that residents and officials of the county took a dim view of the plan, even when, as part of an overall agreement, the Federal government undertook to make "in-lieu" payments to cover the taxes on the 32,000 acres of formerly privately owned lands which the county lost as a result of enlarging the Park. Among the justifiable assumptions was that inasmuch as the National Park Service did not permit grazing on National Park or National Monument lands, cattle ranchers in the Jackson Hole area, who for years had grazed their cattle on National Forest lands which were shortly to be included in the National Monument and National Park, expected that they probably would be denied not only the right to graze on park lands, but even the right to drive their cattle from the Jackson Hole area through the Park to their traditional summer grazing ranges north of the Grand Teton National Park. By special provision in the act enlarging the area of the Grand Teton National Park, an exception was made to permit the continuation of the use of these lands for grazing by these ranchers. It is interesting to note that in the hearings in the early 1940s mention had been made of 16,000 cattle which would be forced off these lands, and that recent studies of the economics of Teton County speak of around

17,000 head of cattle still being grazed. In other words, although the numbers of cattle have not increased materially, they certainly have not dwindled to the disappearing point, as had been prophesied by witnesses at congressional hearings.

Loud among other objectors to the inclusion of the Jackson Hole National Monument in the Grand Teton National Park were the hunters. Their opposition was based on the fact that the National Park Service traditionally banned hunting on park lands, whereas the Forest Service usually permitted it. In the case of the Jackson Hole area the situation was complicated by the fact that the elk, or wapiti, which summered in the Yellowstone region, generally followed a seasonal route of migration into the Jackson Hole area for their winter feed.

Preservation of the elk was one of the main concerns of those who advocated placing the Jackson Hole area within a national park or monument. Even before the transaction was completed, the protectionists arranged for the purchase and maintenance of a hay ranch for the express purpose of helping to feed the migrant elk herd when the snows buried the natural winter feed too deep. As a matter of fact the preservation of this elk herd was and has remained one of the many functions of the Grand Teton National Park. Although the licensing for hunting is in the hands of the Wyoming Game and Fish Commission, the determination of the size of the elk herd and of the size of the annual permitted kill remains in the hands of the U. S. Biological Survey, as does the actual carrying out of the emergency feeding program.

Antagonism to the Park Service and friendliness for the Forest Service are widespread among Westerners, especially cattle ranchers and hunters. As I indicate in Chapter II, the basic differences between the two services with respect to use

of the resources which they control are marked. Often the
Forest Service's application of its doctrine of multiple use
has meant that residents near U. S. Forests have continued
to look on them as available to meet the special needs of
those who for a generation or more have taken for granted
that forest lands near their own holdings are theirs to exploit
as they wish. Legally the attitude is hard to justify, but it had
its roots in the activities and attitudes of the frontiersmen.
It was only natural that pioneer settlers should have first
chance to use the then abundant natural resources on nearby
U.S. forest lands. This tradition is still strong in those areas
of the West which are far from urban and industrial settlements.

It became known as early as 1930 that Mr. John D. Rockefeller, Jr., with full approval of the National Park Service,
was buying up privately owned land in the northern part of
Jackson Hole in order to give it to the Federal government
for ultimate inclusion in the National Park. His interest in
this area dated from 1926 when for the second time he visited
Yellowstone National Park. On that occasion, the superintendent of Yellowstone, Mr. Horace M. Albright, drove Mr.
and Mrs. Rockefeller down through the Jackson Hole region
to see the Grand Tetons. They were struck by the contrast
between the beauty of the mountains and the shoddiness of
the roadside lined with billboards, hot-dog stands, filling stations, and other excrescences of the kind which now deface
almost all parts of most landscapes in the United States. What
had been done already on private holdings would be repeated. Characteristically, Mr. Rockefeller began thinking of
possible ways in which the natural beauties of the area could
be preserved unspoiled. Albright told me that the Rocke-
fellers were especially interested to hear of a meeting which

he, Albright, had attended three years previously at the cabin of Miss Maud Noble in the Jackson Hole area. At this meeting a group of local citizens, including the well-known writer and dude rancher, Struthers Burt, proposed that funds be raised to buy the ranches north of Jackson with the thought that if this purchase could be made it would be easier to include this part of Jackson Hole in a national park. Miss Noble's cabin bears a bronze plaque commemorating this meeting and describing the plan discussed there as "one for setting aside a portion of Jackson Hole as a national recreation area for the use and enjoyment of the people of the United States." The plaque added that "the purpose of that plan has been accomplished by the establishment and enlargement of the Grand Teton National Park. The broad vision and patriotic foresight of those who met here that July evening in 1923 will be increasingly appreciated by our country with the passing years."

According to Albright, Mr. Rockefeller asked him what the probable cost of acquiring the privately owned lands in Jackson Hole would be, and whether the Park Service would accept them as a gift. As the number of plots concerned was considerable it required time to prepare the necessary information, but the following winter Albright furnished Mr. Rockefeller the figures he wanted. Out of this grew the plan to organize the Snake River Land Company to buy at fair value as much as possible of these lands for ultimate transfer to the Park Service. Mr. Rockefeller's connection with the Snake River Land Company was not at first disclosed, to avoid increasing the prices unnaturally and also to prevent suspicion that the lands were being bought by Mr. Rockefeller, not to give to the park, but for the Standard Oil Company to profit from rich deposits of oil (which did not exist).

Wyoming politicians, largely under the influence of cattle ranchers who feared that their grazing privileges might be curtailed, were virulent in their opposition to the whole project. One of them, Congressman Barrett, charged that Albright had deliberately "deceived" the people of Wyoming by failing to state publicly that the purchaser was John D. Rockefeller, Jr. He also charged Albright with having plotted and schemed to acquire these lands for the National Park Service in the face of congressional opposition. Apparently it never occurred to Congressman Barrett that the acquisition of land desirable as parts of parks or monuments is a constant concern of the National Park Service, and that Albright would have been remiss if he had failed to work for the acquisition of lands which he was convinced would be important additions to all existing or proposed parks. As I have already indicated, the National Park Service in its first annual report, published in 1917, urged park status for the Tetons and most of Jackson Hole. Confirmation of the soundness of Mr. Albright's foresight in this case is to be found in the way in which attendance at Grand Teton National Park, which now includes these areas, has been skyrocketing.

I never met Barrett, nor other leaders of the Wyoming opposition, most of whom passed into deserved oblivion years ago. But, as I indicate in Chapter IV, I have known Albright for more than forty years and have worked with him on many conservation problems. To anybody who knows him the charges of "intrigue" and "deception" which were made against him are ridiculous. Albright and the other supporters of the proposal to include the Jackson Hole area in a national park not only fully appreciated the importance of saving it from commercial and urban desecration, but also saw more

clearly the economic benefits to the region of the establishment of the park than did those who opposed it.

As an example of the blindness of the opposition, I quote
from Congressman Barrett's statement before the hearings of
the House Committee on public lands in 1943 in which he
discussed the "inevitable" destruction of the cattle industry
in the area and added: "And in destroying the cattle business
in the country all other business will suffer in proportion.
Merchants, garages, banks, filling stations, professional men,
labor, farm and ranch hands, and many others who are dependent upon the business created by the operations of these
ranches will be seriously affected by this action."

Yet within a few years of the actual incorporation of the
Jackson Hole National Monument into the Grand Teton
National Park, the affairs of Teton County and Jackson un-
derwent such an expansion that a study of the resources, people, and economy of Teton County published in 1967 stated:
"Teton County occupies a very enviable position of strength
in the Wyoming and regional economy," and concluded:
"The potential of continued economic expansion is very
high and Teton can expect a very bright future." This expansion and prosperity was, of course, the direct result of the
successful development of Grand Teton National Park with
the inclusion of the Jackson Hole area which the cattlemen
had so bitterly sought to prevent.

The fact that Jackson has prospered as a result of the final
rounding-out and development of Grand Teton National
Park does not mean that the old-timers who fought the
project no longer have any regrets about the outcome. As the
late Olaus Murie, who lived in Jackson throughout most of
the struggle, explained in his book, *Wapiti Wilderness:* "It
is hard to give up a natural proprietary feeling of ownership

and let the world in." The residents of Jackson had dreaded for years what Murie described as "an 'invasion' of their own chosen valley by government, by tourists, by more and more dudes, by proposals to do this and to do that with the valley." It was *their* valley—not the valley of the National Park Service or of Eastern conservationists.

The residents of the Jackson Hole area were—and still are —strongly aware of the uniqueness of their surroundings, which is more than can be said of many other communities near other sites of great scenic value. Yet their resentment against the "invasion"—much of which was fanned by their distrust of the National Park Service—probably had its roots in the traditional dislike of interference in local affairs by outsiders which is widespread among small-town and rural Americans. It was reinforced by the old-timers' distrust of change, especially of change brought about by policies which they had fought. Both of these reactions have been effectively used in holding conservationists at bay, and yet many conservationists consistently tend to dismiss this opposition as "unreasonable." In many cases this is what it is; but however illogical it may have been, it has delayed many conservation movements and defeated others. Failure to recognize the sensitivity of local groups brought up in this tradition of "hands off" has plagued many conservationists working in behalf of good causes throughout the country.

6

MULTIPLE USE OF THE FORESTS

WHEN the Forest Service was established as a bureau in the Department of Agriculture by President Theodore Roosevelt in 1905 it was charged with stewardship of the natural resources of the National Forest lands. Its function was custodial and its policy utilitarian. Few persons in those days thought that the Service should save scenery or provide for outdoor recreation. Men took scenery for granted. Outdoor recreation, as we know it, was virtually nonexistent. Even most of those who favored making Yellowstone and Yosemite into National Parks to save their magnificent and unique scenery saw little sense in saving less spectacular areas. Unscathed scenery was abundant in the West in the early decades of this century. Even the East still had plenty. (This was, of course, before the birth of bulldozers.) Urbanization was spotty in the early 1900s, where now it is rampant almost everywhere. Suburban sprawl had not begun. Roads were narrow, crooked, and rough. The volume of motor traffic on them was small. Trucking had not yet become profitable. As for wilderness—the country was so full of it that few thought of setting aside wilderness areas posted: "Keep out!"

The work of the Forest Service was practical—to conserve the resources on Forest lands for long-term uses. When needed these resources were to be made available under Forest Service regulation and supervision, and the government was to be paid fair value for their use. To paraphrase Pinchot, the National Forest lands were to provide sustained production of whatever crop or services would be the most useful and were to be put to their most productive uses for the permanent good of the whole people, rather than for the temporary benefit of individuals and corporations.

Pinchot as chief forester emphasized the interrelationship between the logging of forests on a sustained-yield basis, the control of grazing, and the protection of watersheds—each an important function, regionally and nationally. It is pertinent to note here that most of the water used in the Pacific states today has its sources on National Forest lands, and some of it on National Park lands. Pinchot insisted that so long as the forests were cropped rather than stripped they would protect the growth of grass for pasture, which, if not overgrazed, would help impound the runoff of rain and discourage erosion and the silting of streams. Cropped forests would also shelter wildlife, which was desirable not so much because men liked to hunt as because game furnished part of the diet of families living near National Forests. The fact that among visitors to National Forests were a few dreamers who thought that the Forests in time might well be useful for outdoor recreation had little influence on the early shaping of Forest Service policies. The first appropriation for recreation facilities on Forest lands was not made until 1922—seventeen years after the service had been established—and amounted to only

$10,000, which suggests that recreation was of relatively little concern to the Forest Service in those days.

Persons unfamiliar with the conditions and attitudes that prevailed near National Forests in the early 1900s wonder why the Forest Service policy of regulating the use of resources on Forest lands, which now seems so sound, was then so fiercely fought. When the Forest Service began to control the use of natural resources on its lands it knew that there would be opposition and resistance on the part of ranchers, lumbermen, and others who had long been using, or had planned to use, as much as they could of the resources of the Forest lands for their own profit. But Washington officials did not foresee the intensity of the state-wide determination in most Western states that local politicians rather than Washington bureaucrats should prescribe the uses of resources on National Forest lands. The Forest Service took the simple and logical position that as Congress had given it jurisdiction over the National Forests, the manner of use of the Forest resources was a Federal responsibility to be carried out in the interest of the nation as a whole, and not a local function to be performed by, and in the primary interest of, local residents. In other words, the issue between the Forest Service and the Western states sixty years ago was not *use* but *control*. Neither group wanted to lock up the Forest resources forever. Most local opponents of the Forest Service's stewardship of the natural resources on the National Forests were even more frankly utilitarian than was Pinchot. They fought Federal control because it meant regulation, which, in turn, made restrictions on use possible, with the clear implication that use could even be denied. There is irony in the fact that Pinchot, whom Westerners attacked so bitterly because he favored control of Forest resources, was berated by Eastern preservationists because, as a utilitarian, he expected that the resources on National Forest lands would ultimately be useful. Westerners wanted no control. Easterners wanted no use.

In fairness to Pinchot it should be said that if he had shared the preservationists' policy of nonuse it is unlikely that he could have done as much for conservation as, in fact, he did as an avowed utilitarian. Congress almost surely would have scalped him. Even though most congressmen shared Pinchot's utilitarian views, they distrusted him as a theorist, feared him as a trained expert, and resented his building up a corps of professionally trained forest rangers and supervisers to take the place of incompetent and usually uninformed political hacks, who till then had had charge of Forest lands. Furthermore, as he was a close friend and protégé of Theodore Roosevelt, whose independence, and often defiance, of Congress irked members of that body, congressmen were glad to snipe at Pinchot, hoping thus to annoy, and perhaps even to thwart, the President whom so many of them hated.

Stewardship of the natural resources on National Forest lands led to the concept which was given a label of which the Forest Service has long been proud: "multiple use." This once vague phrase, now clarified, covers a variety of operations. The best definition—because the simplest—describes multiple use as "managing the nation's forest resources for sustained yields of wood, water, forage, wildlife and recreation." The Forest lands were to be used on a permanent, rather than a short-term basis. Through research, cooperation with the states and with private forest owners, and experience in managing national forests and grasslands, the Forest Service set out to increase its usefulness to the nation— usefulness through reducing erosion and floods, protecting the courses of water from damage, and encouraging tree growth and a good cover of brush and grass so as to check runoff.

Still further amplification of the doctrine of multiple use is to be found in the wording of the act of Congress dated June 12, 1960, which states that "the National Forests are established and shall be administered for outdoor recreation, range, timber, watershed, wildlife and fish purposes." Multiple use is specifically defined as meaning "the management of all the various renewable surface resources of the National Forests so that they are utilized in the combination that will best meet the needs of the American people; making the most judicious use of the land for some or all of these related resources or services over areas large enough to provide sufficient latitude for possible adjustment in use to conform to changing needs and conditions; that some land will be used for less than all of the resources; and harmonious and coordinated management of the various resources, each with the other, without impairment of the productivity of the land with consideration being given to the relative values of the various resources, and not necessarily the combination of uses that will give the greatest dollar return or the greatest unit output." Which is congressionalese for saying: "Plan and use wisely."

As the Forest Service, besides stressing multiple use, refers frequently to "sustained yield," it is pertinent to note that this phrase also is defined in this act of Congress as follows: "Sustained yield of the several products and services means the achievement and maintenance in perpetuity of a high-level annual or regular periodic output of the various removable resources of the National Forests without impairment of the productivity of the land." In other words, use, but do not use up, the Forests' natural resources.

In Chapter VII I discuss various aspects of the conflicts inherent in the implementation of the concept of wilderness. Here it is pertinent to note that officials in the Forest Service believe that the latest congressional revision of legislation pertaining to wilderness areas—the so-called Wilderness Act of 1964—may be useful in facilitating the permanent preservation of some of the more scenic areas in the National Forests from ultimate commercial development.

The term "multiple use" does not suggest that any one particular use, such as the logging of designated forest areas under supervision necessarily either precludes other uses or takes precedence over them. A half century ago the main concern of the Forest Service was with the supervision and control of extractive operations, but since that time the Service has become the largest single purveyor of recreation facilities in the country. The number of visitors to the National Forests in search of recreation continues to increase. Both of these uses of the Forest lands—logging and recreation—are not only lawful but are of major concern to the Service. While they are not necessarily mutually exclusive they can certainly be incompatible. A half century ago priority would almost surely have been given to lumbering. Is there any valid reason why priority today should not be given to recreation? Any such inclination on the part of the Forest Service would, of course, meet with bitter opposition. Competition for use of Forest lands is sure to increase and will come primarily from individuals and groups eager to exploit the resources on these lands for their own profit. The mere fact that the doctrine of "multiple use" has, in the long run, been flexible, implies that the great interest of the service in recreation is likely to incline it to discourage commercial invasions. For years the Forest Service has been studying possibilities for the more effective use of its reserves of recreation lands. But such a policy on the part of the service is sure to be systematically opposed by the "Big Three" of Western business—the lumber, grazing, and mining interests. It would not be surprising if such opposition would stiffen the Forest Service to protect its obligations in connection with recreation from commercial would-be users of natural resources on lands which the Forest Service believes would serve a better purpose if dedicated to recreation.

The extraordinary growth of the furnishing of recreational facilities on National Forest lands by the Forest Service is dramatically brought out in the figures of use of the Forests for recreation purposes. These show that in 1925 the Service listed the total number of visits to all forests for recreation purposes in that year to be a little more than 5,600,000. In 1964 total visits to all of the National Forests for the same period increased about twenty-five fold. An interesting confirmation of the unexpectedly fast growth of the number of visitors to the National Forests for recreation purposes is that in 1957 the Forest Service estimated that by 1975 they might reach 135,000,000, whereas this figure was, in fact, approximated in 1965—ten years ahead of the anticipated date. In other words, public use of forest lands for recreation purposes has grown much more rapidly than the experts had expected.

Of perhaps even greater significance as an indication of the importance which the Forest Service attaches to recreation is the fact that by the mid-sixties the Forest Service operated more than half of all the developed campsites in the United States. The Outdoor Recreation Resources Review Commission (ORRRC) report, which published this fact, in 1963 also noted that about 70 per cent of all public lands dedicated to recreation uses at that time were in the National Forests. Fully as significant is the statement in the Forest Service's own analysis of the recreation potentials on National Forest lands, published in 1965, to the effect that "the recreation resources of the National Forests can be developed and managed skillfully enough to meet most of the demands upon them ending well into the next century." Such a statement coming from this particular branch of the government suggests that the total acreage of as yet undeveloped but already earmarked recreation areas within the National Forests is very large.

As the need for recreation facilities increases it is to be hoped that conservation leaders in and out of the government will give due weight to the fact that recreation is closely associated with and dependent upon environment, and that one of the most important aspects of environment is its scenic values. Scenery—which has always been limited geographically—is being destroyed, outside of National Parks and National Forests, at an ever faster pace, by the three great consumers of land and landscape—real-estate promoters, industrial developers, and highway engineers. Environment, landscape, and scenery are regarded by these destroyers as potential obstacles to "progress." The only scale of values which they respect is economic: Will a project pay, or will it either cost too much to prepare or bring in too little revenue? Only if it is not likely to be profitable is there any chance that the planned destruction of the environment can be prevented.

The net result of wanton destruction of scenery on nongovernmental lands has been to give scarcity values to landscape, environment, and scenery. The more crudely and extensively scenery is destroyed on private holdings, the greater is the importance of protecting scenic areas on public lands.

Scenery is not a renewable resource. There is no sound reason why on government-owned lands economic values need be given greater weight than recreational and scenic values. The mere fact that in numerous instances the Federal government itself has facilitated the development of commercial projects in areas of exceptional scenic interest—such as the building of dams along the Colorado River—does not mean that such a mistaken policy should be continued indefinitely. Except on government reserves such as parks and forests, regardless of what level of government administers them, environment is at the mercy of men with bulldozers.

As a result the responsibility which rests on the Federal, state, and local governments to help preserve the scenic values on public lands has increased enormously. If environment is worth preserving—as all civilized persons believe to be the case—recreation, with all that it means in human values, may become a fruitful ally in supporting the cause of preservation. All things point to a steadily increasing demand for outdoor recreation facilities in agreeable surroundings. If we cannot cry "Halt!" to the destroying of private lands, government at least can say to the men with the bulldozers: "Hitherto shall ye come, but no further!" If we continue to do this with the active support of the U. S. Forest Service we shall have won victory in retreat, and the service will have added to multiple use the highly important achievement of saving scenery for the ages.

The details of the work of the Forest Service would fill volumes. It is only necessary here to note a few, most of which center on planning for long-range use such as construction of roads, not only for public use but also to provide access in case of fire; the recreation development projects; the maintenance and policing of public campgrounds, picnic sites, roads, and trails, and, of course, prevention and suppression of fire. This last function is so vast that it will be described in detail in a separate chapter. Relations with the public are extensive and complicated, inasmuch as the public includes lumber companies which now harvest billions of feet of National Forest lumber under contract; hundreds of thousands of hunters and fishermen; tens of millions of campers, picknickers, and other vacationers, as well as bird-watchers, photographers, skiiers, hikers, and rock-hounds and—in some ways the most difficult of all—the many thousands of persons owning or leasing private property within National Forests boundaries obtained before the present had been established. It has been estimated that of the 186,000,000 acres within the National Forest about 40,000,000 acres are still in other hands. As in the case of National Park lands (see Chapter IV) these so-called "inholdings" often present serious problems. In the second half of the nineteenth century, alternate sections of public lands were granted to the railroads to encourage them to build, but there are still endless problems in connection with boundaries, the location and maintenance of roads, telegraph and power lines. Confusion arises from the original crazy concept of checkerboarding in alternate square miles of government and privately owned lands to a distance of twenty miles from the right of way. Most of these lands were inadequately surveyed, and due to the checkerboard pattern, have blocked both private and government projects. This scheme, which Congress evolved in a relatively few debates, has taken decades to unscramble and is still responsible for lengthy and complicated negotiations between the government and private interests trying to consolidate areas by exchange or by purchase and sale.

The details of how the Forest Service handles its millions

of visitors do not concern us here. Suffice it to say that an enormous amount of constructive thought has been and continues to be given by the Forest Service to the best ways of enabling the American public to enjoy the recreational facilities on the Forest lands. Ample information is available to the public, simply presented, in comprehensive leaflets and pamphlets about almost all the recreational facilities which the Forest Service has under its care. This bureau has a fine history of constructive work in many fields of conservation and is constantly studying new ways in which it can serve the public. No longer is recreation a side issue. It is now of concern to many millions of persons, thanks in no small degree to the effective work of the Forest Service in opening up Forest lands for recreation. As one who knew many of the early figures in the work of developing the Forest resources, my guess is that if Theodore Roosevelt, Gifford Pinchot, and his successors as director of the Forest Service could see the imaginative work of that service in these fields since their day they would say: "Well done!"

7

WHAT WILDERNESS?

Most conservationists agree that wilderness should be saved, but they are at odds about the "Whats," the "Whys," and the "Hows." Furthermore, they fail to distinguish between *a* wilderness, and *the* wilderness. To most people *a* wilderness connotes a rugged, remote region, rarely visited and as yet undefiled by civilization. *The* wilderness, in contrast, usually refers not to an area but to the state of nature that prevailed throughout the North American continent before the arrival of white men. The confusion resulting from the two meanings of the word has been enhanced by the fact that little remains of the original wilderness other than a few portions in the Appalachian Mountains and in the Rockies and the Pacific Northwest. Furthermore, most of the wilderness areas inside of the Wilderness Preservation System are mere fragments—scattered remnants—of the original American wilderness which are still intact because they were hard to reach. They are typical of only the rougher portions of the original wilderness out of which most of the America of today was carved.

The meaning of wilderness has also been confused by a strange sort of romanticism which has its roots in the writings of Rousseau, Chateaubriand, and other French authors just before the outbreak of the French Revolution—men who were fascinated by the idea of "back to nature." Underlying their philosophy was the quaint notion that if urban intellectuals could spend a few days in the bayous of Louisiana and the lower Mississippi they would be spiritually purged through contacts with nature in the raw. In the middle of the nineteenth century, thanks largely to the writings of James Fenimore Cooper, whose famous "leatherstocking," Natty Bumppo, seemed to be a noble child of the wilderness, American intellectuals inclined towards Cooper's assumption that the wilderness fostered nobility of character. When the grandparents of present-day Americans were growing up, they fell heir to a similar illusion—or delusion—which inhered in the tales and verses setting forth the triumphs of man alone in the wilderness: the writings of Jack London (*The Call of the Wild*), the animal tales of Stewart Edward White, and the verses of Robert W. Service (*The Spell of the Yukon*), in all of which a bout with the wilderness cured men of their weaknesses. On a more sophisticated level, and with greater literary skill, Rudyard Kipling romanticized the prophylactic qualities of nature in his tales of the sea and the jungle. He had deeper understanding than these other three, and greater perspicacity, especially when he wrote the verses about "something lost behind the ranges." More recently current writers have revived the theory that American pioneers drew strength from the wilderness.

As a one-time student in Frederick Jackson Turner's class

on the influence of the frontier on American history, I question this oft-repeated concept of the spiritual influence of the
wilderness on the American people. It is true that the westward trek was epic, and that the men—and particularly the
women—who crossed much of the continent on foot were a
tough breed. But they won out not because the wilderness
had given them spiritual strength, but because they had overcome and destroyed the wilderness. Their physical endurance
was fortified by the vast amount of labor they had to perform
in order to survive and not because of imaginary forces sup-
posedly spawned by the wilderness that they had fought. Instead of inspiring them the wilderness embittered them. To
farm they had first to clear the forest. They could not build
without felling trees, either for lumber or for log cabins.
They were at the mercy of the seasons and of the weather,
and as they moved westward the prairie sod resisted—and
sometimes even twisted—their plows. Farther west the drier
lands parched their crops and scorched their stock. They en-
dured thirst and hunger, but many of the weak fell by the
wayside.

Advocates of preserving wilderness areas have often emphasized the value of remoteness. To the extent that remoteness means "hard to reach" the argument is sound. But a
hiker may find a small, accessible, but well-secluded area and
enjoy it. Conversely, he could be absolutely isolated in the
midst of a vast forest and yet be so hemmed in by trees and
undergrowth that the experience would be unrewarding. In
the final analysis enjoyment of a wilderness area depends on
what we see. Scenic values, obviously, are hard to define.
They include spectacular formations such as the Grand Canyon of the Colorado, the geysers in Yellowstone, and Rainbow Natural Bridge, as well as conspicuous mountain ranges

such as Mount Rainier and Mount Hood, and deep valleys such as Yosemite, and, until "civilization" destroyed it, Hetch Hetchy. Yet Americans of today and tomorrow owe a great debt to the little band of men of vision who, beginning about a century ago, believed that some of these natural phenomena were of permanent value to the nation as a whole in their present condition and must be placed under the protective custody of the Federal government in order to insure their preservation.

It was my good fortune to have known one of the old timers who not only was tough and long lived, but who had played a big part in the early days of the conservation movement in the United States. This was William Henry Jackson, who had a keen eye for scenery and who visited the Yellowstone area in 1869. He happened to be a great photographer as well, and his photographs of Yellowstone did much to influence Congress to pass the legislation setting aside the Yellowstone area as a national park.

Wiry and alert despite his age of ninety-nine when I met him, he told me that he had driven across the continent by covered wagon; that he had ridden horseback from the Mississippi to the Coast; that he had crossed the continent by train and by automobile, and had flown over much of it. Then he paused and said he had still one great ambition before he died and that was to make a nonstop flight by plane from coast to coast. A few weeks later he fell, broke his hip, and died.

The work of William Henry Jackson and others, to persuade Congress to set aside Yellowstone as a national park long before the National Park Service and the U.S. Forest Service had even been thought of, was, in a sense, a forerunner of the present interest in giving greater protection to wilderness areas. Yellowstone, like Yosemite, was so spectacular that it was in danger of being overrun and defaced by an uncontrolled public, abetted by commercial exploiters. The area had to be saved and protected, but as there were then no national parks and few restrictions on the use of public land, custodianship and preservation of Yellowstone was hard to formulate. The solution was to turn over the region in 1886 to the Army, which still had forts through the West in case of Indian trouble. The immediate objective was to prevent further destruction of the area, even though no one foresaw that the number of visitors would increase so fast and soon that the park which was being set aside for people to enjoy would soon be in danger of destruction by the careless feet and grasping hands of visitors.

The purpose of setting aside both Yellowstone and Yosemite was, of course, to save their scenery. Jackson's role was to bring this scenery to the eyes of congressmen who had never visited Yellowstone. Had these early national parks not been established, they and other specimens of spectacular scenery would almost surely have been lost. While none of the areas now being included in the Wilderness Preservation System are comparable in scenic value to the more spectacular parts of the Yellowstone and Yosemite, their designation by act of Congress as part of the National Wilderness Preservation System will make it more difficult for commercial interests to raid them for profit. The Wilderness Act of 1964 has loopholes, but it also has provisions for preserving areas that should be saved, and even though the provisions of the Act are by no means comprehensive the policy may prove effective.

The wilderness concept is relatively new. It is true that in the organic act establishing the National Parks, the injunction to maintain them in their natural condition was equivalent to saying that they should be kept as wilderness areas. The first area actually set aside as wilderness—the Gila Wilderness Area in the Gila National Forest in New Mexico—was established by the Forest Service in 1924, largely under the inspiration of Aldo Leopold. Although Leopold is generally credited with having been the prime sponsor of the wilderness concept, another forest ranger, Arthur Carhart, had been interested in wilderness and had talked and corresponded with Leopold about it. Leopold contended that wilderness was as much a natural resource as are trees and pasture. A few years later Robert Marshall also became greatly interested in wilderness areas and until his early death, did much for the wilderness preservation movement. The actual sequence of events in the development of wilderness areas does not concern us here, but of great importance is the fact that able and clear-headed men in the Forest Service induced their superiors to establish such areas, which in those days was done by administrative order. Under their impetus the Forest Service became deeply involved in the preservation of wilderness areas. During the last forty years it has done more than any Federal bureau to set aside and protect wilderness. Designation of wilderness areas was set forth in official directives, of which the first was L-20, issued in 1929, and had as its purpose to preserve "primitive conditions of environment, transportation, habitation and subsistence within the national forests." Three areas were set aside in 1930, and within the next nine years a total of seventy-eight areas were designated formally by the Forest Service as "primitive areas," totalling 13,644,599 acres. In 1929 two new Forest Service regulations were issued setting forth the procedures to be followed in the establishing of primitive areas. Under regulation U-1 a new label, "wilderness area," was applied to areas of 100,000 acres or more, and under U-2 so-called "wild" areas were classed as comprising more than 5,000 but less than 100,000 acres.

In 1964 Congress passed the Wilderness Act which established the National Wilderness Preservation System. The new Act requires congressional designation of wilderness areas after congressional hearings, which, be it noted, easily could play into the hands of the opponents of conservation. All forest areas classified as "wilderness" or "wild" areas in 1964 were incorporated in the new Wilderness Preservation System on the effective date of the Wilderness Act. The Boundary Waters Canoe Area in Minnesota has also been included in the Wilderness System. Under a special provision of the Act, re-examination of all primitive and roadless areas is being made and the recommendations of the agency reviewing them for their inclusion in the wilderness system must be approved by Congress.

The Wilderness Act implements previous legislation and includes a definition of wilderness as "an area where the earth and its community of life are untrammelled by man, where man himself is a visitor who does not remain . . . an area of undeveloped Federal land retaining its primeval character and influence without permanent improvement or human habitation, which is protected and managed so as to preserve its natural condition." It also notes that such areas must have "outstanding opportunities for solitude or a primitive and unconfined type of recreation." The Act further specifies that "there shall be no commercial enterprise and no permanent road within any wilderness area designated by this Act," as well as no use of motorized equipment, motorboats or aircraft. This presumably would prevent all kinds of commercial development.

Unfortunately, these commendable provisions are linked with others of a more questionable nature. To begin with, these restrictions are subject to exemptions for existing private rights. Prospecting for minerals is permitted up to midnight, December 31, 1983. "Prospecting for water resources, the establishment and maintenance of reservoirs, water conservation works, power projects, transmission lines and other facilities needed in the public interest, including the construction and maintenance essential to development and use thereof" may be authorized by the President. To a layman these would appear to be very large loopholes. In the case of valid mining claims it is expressly stated that the "Secretary of Agriculture shall, by reasonable regulation, consistent with the preservation of the area as wilderness, permit ingress and egress to such surrounded areas by means which have been or are being enjoyed with respect to other areas similarly situated." While this applies presumably to private lands within the borders of a wilderness area, it is clear that the protection, while greater than any that had existed hitherto, must still be regarded as somewhat tenuous. It is not too cynical to suggest that if the Wilderness Act can be used to help preserve from commercial development some of the particularly fine scenic areas within the National Forests which have not yet been opened to commercial development the reason is more likely to be because these areas are inaccessible, or the high cost of developing them would be prohibitive rather than because the regions have been under the protective custody of the Forest Service. This, be it noted, is in no sense a criticism of the service. Rather is it a recognition of the indisputable fact that as in so many other instances in the growth of the American governmental system legislation has been the result of compromises between conflicting interests and claims.

The mechanics of preserving wilderness areas are complicated. In the first place, too many visitors can ruin them. As it would be unreasonable to close the wilderness areas to all visitors, the Forest Service faces the working out of a compromise between the two extremes. The Wilderness Act of 1964 states that wilderness areas shall be closed to all motorized traffic except for administrative purposes in connection with fire suppression and emergencies involving the public safety. This is an important and constructive control of use. But this need not prevent the Forest Service from providing substantial parking areas and facilities for camping, and even cabins available for overnight occupancy just outside of wilderness areas. From such points of entry into a wilderness area there could be a reasonably broad trail which would be used by a substantial, but necessarily limited, number of visitors. These main trails could connect with a series of narrow dirt trails leading to overlooks or other interesting spots. These smaller trails could be of two classes: 1) for the general public; and 2) for hardened hikers. This second category of trails could be modeled on the technique devised by Colonel John R. White, superintendent of Sequoia National Park, a half century ago, when he sought to discourage inexperienced hikers from taking trails into areas where they might get lost or panic. White's system, as I describe in Chapter I, was to make the first quarter mile of such trails so steep and rough as to discourage all but seasoned hikers. It is conceivable that overnight camping accommodations of a primitive kind could be located within wilderness areas for experienced hikers without serious damage to the wilderness aspect of the area.

The purpose of such campsites would be to enable back-packers to enjoy the wilderness to the full. The chances are that if the trails were skillfully engineered they would discourage all but the hardiest and most experienced hikers, and so would automatically help to prevent the areas from being overrun.

To avoid overcrowding is as important as it is difficult. Most visitors to wilderness areas hope to escape crowds. Whether alone or in groups of friends they want to be able to hike through wilderness without being disturbed by the noises of other hikers—the blare of transistors or the loud shouting of one hiker to another, and similar distractions. They feel, and rightly, that one of the chief values of wilderness is that it offers escape from the noises of our modern mechanized, overcrowded world. The conclusion is clear that to admit too many visitors to a wilderness area at the same time can deprive such an area of one of its major values.

The changes which have occurred in the attitude as well as the functions of the Forest Service in the last fifty years suggest that the service will find satisfactory solutions for this problem. Today most foresters regard the maintenance of wilderness as a sound use of forest lands. So, in time, they will surely consider the preservation of scenery for the benefit and enjoyment of vacationists as a proper facet of multiple use. In fact, it may be predicted that the greater the destruction of scenery by bulldozers on private lands the greater will be the appreciation of scenery on public lands, and the greater will be the attention which the service will have to give to its preservation.

The saving of scenery on public land will almost surely meet with the hostility of processors eager to resist extensions of government control over any category of public lands. It is therefore almost certain that they will oppose all plans for protecting wilderness areas from attempted incursions by the extractive industries. The cleavage between the local residents and the Federal government about the use of public lands has been deep for decades.

As I suggested in the preceding chapter, the Forest Service is not committed to favor any particular one of the multiple uses of the resources of forest lands over others. Until such time as recreation was accepted as a major resource of the forest lands the service was inclined to give priority to extraction and removal of physical resources. This suggests that nowadays, when the Service's preoccupation with recreation and with the preservation of wilderness areas is so great, it would be acting according to its tradition by giving greater weight than heretofore to uses of forest lands for the benefit and enjoyment of the steadily increasing number of visitors from all parts of the country in search of recreation. In the event that commercial interests try to win congressional support for changing existing laws so as to make it easier to exploit resources now protected in wilderness areas, it would be in keeping with the service's policy of multiple use to look on recreational uses of the forests as deserving special consideration and protection.

The Forest Service has for years been criticized by conservationists not for failing to implement its policies but for attempting to carry out the long-range policies of stewardship with which it was originally charged. It is easy enough to criticize particular actions of the Forest Service. But in fairness to the overall work of the organization for more than sixty years it should be noted that under the policies with which the service was originally charged and which were modified from time to time by congressional and administrative actions, it has done an admirable job. Many of us regret that it was not initially charged not only with powers, but also with the mandate, to preserve larger areas under lock and key. But the service is an agent, not a principal. Had it not done everything possible to carry out its responsibilities the nation today would have a smaller area of public lands for recreation or for any other purposes.

FIGHTING FOREST FIRES

THE United States Forest Service is responsible for suppressing fires within all National Forests and grasslands. Obviously the service should do what it can to *prevent* fires, but as there are only two sources of forest fires—lightning, and its human counterpart, carelessness, neither of which can be fully controlled—the Forest Service concentrates on quick detection, and when the start of a fire has been reported to headquarters, on prompt suppression before it gets out of hand.

Although the proportion of lightning-caused fires to man-caused fires varies from year to year and region to region, the *Annual Fire Report* for the Calendar Year of 1967, published by the Forest Service, shows that in the five-year period 1962–66, lightning-caused fires averaged 52 per cent and man-caused fires 48 per cent. In the very bad lightning year of 1967 approximately 58 per cent of all forest fires in the National Forests were caused by lightning.

Even though it is not possible to prevent all forest fires, the Forest Service does its best to impress on the public the need of reducing man-caused fires. It has even tried the technique of exaggerating the relative proportion of man-caused fires in some of the Forest Service leaflets handed out to the public. The fact that lightning starts about half of the forest fires in no way lessens the need for doing everything possible to convince visitors to all forests that they must be very careful in any and all uses of fire and of matches. All visitors should be informed that nearly one third of the man-caused fires in National Forests are traceable to smokers, and that almost half are due to careless use of power tools and other mechanical instruments. The danger of carelessness both in discarding cigarette butts and matches and in lighting and using camp fires needs constant re-emphasis. Educating the public will become increasingly important as the numbers of visitors to the forests from urban and suburban areas grow. Most visitors have had no experience with fire in very dry weather and in highly flammable surroundings. Even those who were brought up in suburban residential tracts think in terms of burning trash on a driveway lined with a clipped lawn. They are usually unaware of the ease with which a fire can get out of hand in a dry forest on a hot day.

Education can help cut the number of man-caused forest fires, but the major problem of the Forest Service is, and will remain, how to expedite detection of fires and to devise means to hit a fire early and hard. I talked at length with William H. Hansen, superintendent of the Los Padres National Forest, about this aspect of fire fighting. He explained to me that because of the rough topography in most National Forests, many fires are of considerable size before smoke rises high enough to be seen by the lookouts. This has led the Forest Service to place particular value on the cooperation of the public in reporting fires promptly whenever they see signs of smoke, rather than to assume that someone already has reported this fire. But the Forest Service has, of course, continued to develop its extensive system of lookouts in each National Forest and in addition, is using helicopters in increasing numbers because of their mobility, even though the strong winds that often accompany forest fires can hamper their effectiveness. Helicopters are useful for moving men and equipment quickly to places otherwise inaccessible, especially with an ever-increasing number of helispots established throughout National Forests. In addition, the Forest Service is increasing the use of airplanes to drop slurry, the thin mixture composed of retardant and water, which helps check and even choke hot fires. Planes are also used to drop smoke jumpers.

The lookout is an observation post linked with Forest headquarters by radio or telephone. Its duty is to watch for signs of smoke. A heliport is a developed area where several helicopters can land and be serviced or loaded at the same time. A helispot is a level cleared spot about forty to fifty feet square on which a single 'copter can unload or load. A smokejumper is a firefighter trained to jump with a parachute from a moving plane so that he can reach the ground near a desirable spot from which to attack an approaching fire—a spot which would otherwise be inaccessible. As fuel breaks cannot be explained briefly I shall deal with them below.

In planning to fight fire in National Forests, knowledge of the lay of the land is, of course, essential. Thanks to improved mapping techniques and to aerial photography, excellent, accurate maps of almost all the National Forests, with the possible exception of some in Alaska, are now available. Thoroughly familiar with the maps, the Forest supervisor and his staff often fly over the region under their care and, of course, travel extensively through it. One of their concerns is to find new sites for heliports and helispots, especially in the more remote regions, so as to facilitate prompt detection of fires and quick access for fire fighters.

One of the effective devices for controlling fires in National Forests in California and other critical areas is the building of a network of what the rangers call "fuel breaks." These are so placed that they can help to check a fire, and with speed and luck on the part of the fire fighters, contain it. To persons not in the Forest Service the term "fuel break" is likely to be a puzzler, whereas to the rangers it is clear and logical. Confusion exists because civilians think of fuel as something to add to a fire to make it burn, whereas to Forest Rangers fuel is ground cover of all kinds—including trees—all of which make up what might be called the raw materials of forest fires. Some ground cover, like dry grass, ignites instantly and spreads explosively, and offers little resistance to control efforts. Fire in grass can often be stopped with a narrow fire line stripped to mineral soil, or by small quantities of water expertly applied. Different kinds of brush burn with different intensities. Dense stands of *manzanita* and *ceanothus* ignite readily and burn with fierce heat, so great as to ignite other fuels many feet distant and to threaten the very lives of fire fighters. Large quantities of water are required to cool these fuels below the kindling point. A fire barrier, to be effective, must be several hundred feet wide composed of fuel that fire fighters can control with safety to themselves. The width of a fuel break is determined in part by the nature of the original ground cover. It is a corridor 200 to 500 feet wide that cuts through a continuous area of natural fuel of known burning habits. The native vegetation is deliberately changed by the introduction of plant material of light fuel volume.

The ideal ground cover in a fuel break stops erosion and does not ignite easily or burn too fast or spread sparks. Short perennial grasses which stay green are best. Fuel breaks are intended to change the character of the natural growth of the strip by the introduction of low-growing vegetation that will prevent erosion but has a small heat output if it burns. The purpose is to make it easier to suppress a fire when it reaches a fuel break. But no fire is automatically controlled by a fuel break. It still has to be fought, but fought under reasonably favorable conditions. Hot fires backed by strong winds whisk burning snags by air across a break to start new fires. During the great Sundance fire in Idaho in 1967 burning cones and branches were blown for miles by the strong winds caused by the heat of the fire. But in many kinds of terrain, and in fires which can be fought and checked quickly, fuel breaks have been so effective that their construction has become standard practice in many parts of the country. They are often used on the crests of ridges, where their main function is to discourage or prevent fire from starting down the lee side of the ridge.

Inside of some fuel breaks is what is called a "firebreak." This is a cleared strip usually four to ten feet in width which in the fire season is cleared down to the mineral soil (i.e., below dried vegetation). Fuel breaks and firebreaks are skillfully adapted to the terrain. Their planning, construction, and improvement have been major concerns of the Forest Service, especially between fire seasons.

Fire fighters agree that fighting forest fires can only be learned by experience, but the effectiveness of the work of fire fighters depends in part on good training, advance planning, and on support from headquarters. This, in turn, calls for much advance study and organization. It presupposes, besides knowledge of fire behavior under different weather conditions, understanding of the terrain and its fuels by the Forest personnel. Adequate supplies of mechanical assistance such as bulldozers, helicopters, and airplanes must be immediately available and properly operated.

As the danger of fire increases in very dry years, during long spells of high temperature, and low humidity, and strong winds, reliable knowledge of the atmospheric conditions in the preceding days and weeks is important, as are forecasts of the weather that lies ahead, particularly forecasts of probable temperature and relative humidity. Knowledge of recent weather is often as useful as forecasts. If, for example, rainfall has been below normal for long periods, the danger of a fire spreading increases. So also, if current humidity is very low, a fire will burn faster and be harder to control.

An interesting example of what can happen even under favorable circumstances, when accurate information about relative humidity is lacking, occurred several years ago when a so-called "controlled burn" (burning of brush and grass on private land under the supervision of the State Division of Forestry) was authorized during the dry season on a small plot of privately owned land near the mouth of the Carmel Valley in California. I happened to drive by as the "burn" was started. As my own hygrometer, a quarter mile from the ocean, showed that the relative humidity was very low I felt sure that this "controlled burn" on the hot inland would quickly get out of control—which it did. Although the fire was checked before doing much damage it endangered residences in the Valley and almost jumped into nearby National Forest lands.

Some of us who resented the authorization of a controlled burn on such a very dry, hot day, attended a public hearing under the auspices of the State Division of Forestry the following week. When I asked the ranger who had authorized the burn whether he had checked the relative humidity before the fire was started, he said that he had no instruments for measuring the relative humidity, as no funds had been appropriated for their purchase. He volunteered that he had telephoned to the Hopkins Marine Laboratory, which overlooks Monterey Bay and is exposed to the moist, cooling winds blowing in from the Pacific. The Laboratory reported that the relative humidity there was 85 per cent, which meant that, at least on the shore of Monterey Bay, it would be safe to burn. When I pointed out that the atmospheric conditions on the beach of Monterey Bay bore no relation to the atmospheric conditions in the Carmel Valley, five miles to the south and inland, cut off by high hills from the ocean's moist winds, the ranger said that my point was valid, but he fell back on the bureaucratic explanation that his station did not have the necessary equipment to take a reading of the relative humidity. Some of us protested that such a deficiency in the ranger station's equipment must be corrected—as, in fact, was done in a short time. Clearly it was as unfair to the ranger as to the public to expect him to issue permits for a controlled burn when he lacked the necessary equipment to determine whether the weather was too dry to start such a burn without the danger of the blaze getting out of hand.

Fighting forest fires is a highly specialized occupation, largely dependent on the fire fighters' experience, knowledge, courage, and endurance. Because experience in fighting fire is of prime importance in determining a ranger's effectiveness, all employees in the National Forests are classified according to the actual number of fires in which they have participated. Each member of the Forest Service has a so-called "red card," on which his fire-fighting record and his official position in the fire-fighting hierarchy in the U. S. Forest Service is recorded. In each National Forest this information is tabulated and fire-fighting crews are designated in advance of the season, ready to start without delay.

In order to be designated to perform certain jobs such as "fire boss," "line boss," and "plans chief," the men who control the actual operations of suppressing a fire must have fought at least thirty fires of which ten were large project fires. Without extensive experience few, if any, forest fire fighters are given leading positions of responsibility on the line of fire.

The service also has the well-established practice of holding what might be termed post-mortems after a fire of substantial intensity has been suppressed. At these sessions men who have taken part discuss aspects of this particular operation and exchange ideas about possible alternative moves which might have been helpful or which might be tried in another fire on similar terrain and with similar temperature and wind conditions. They also consider possible changes in tactics which might be made in any particular phase of fire fighting. Although the discussions are, in a sense, theoretical, they help even experienced firefighters to learn useful points about their profession in which so many unexpected and often uncontrollable incidents may require completely different techniques of attack.

All the men of experience in fighting fires with whom I have talked are in agreement about the great importance of being able to spot a fire instantly and to start fighting it before it gets a chance to become hot. That this is not mere theory may be judged from the fact that when the Sisar Canyon fire started near the Ojai Valley in California on October

29, 1967, the first report of the fire reached the Forest head-quarters at 10:27 A.M. on that date. The Forest supervisor told me that the first squad of fire fighters left at 10:28 A.M.—just one minute later—and reached the scene of the fire in six minutes. Seven minutes after this a follow-up squad was dispatched to help the first crew of fire fighters. Such almost instantaneous action is only possible when there has been intensive planning by a highly competent staff.

More complicated than dispatching men by truck or helicopter is the mobilization of equipment for immediate use in emergencies—bulldozers, helicopters, airplanes, etc. Each Forest has a limited supply of government-owned equipment which means that when more is needed units either are borrowed from other Forests or are rented. As the extra equipment must be immediately available it cannot be too far from the scene of the fire. Furthermore, it is essential that the equipment be operated by drivers or pilots familiar with fire fighting. Serious complications may arise when *two or more* fires start at about the same time in nearby areas during a period of high temperatures, low humidity, and strong winds.

Due to the increasing use of helicopters most Forests are looking for new sites for helispots so as to be able to land helicopters where the crews and supplies are most needed. These helispots also facilitate the delivery of food, water and other equipment. Just as the use of helicopters has steadily increased so has the use of planes to fly over fires and drop what the rangers call retardants, which, as I have explained, help to check the spread of fires. This kind of flying is highly specialized and not only requires planes equipped to carry the liquid which is dumped on fires, but also must be piloted by men who know from experience how far above a fire they should fly, and just when to drop their load of slurry. They must also be familiar with the flying hazards over hot fires due to violent up-and-down drafts.

It is unwise to generalize from a single instance of successful quick suppression that there is a particular plan of attack that is more likely to be effective than others. But the official summary of the suppression of the Sisar Canyon fire may be enlightening to persons who have had no experience in fighting fires. The concluding paragraph of the report reads: "It is the considered judgment of those involved in control of the Sisar fire that (1) Without the fuel breaks; (2) Without the immediate strong sustained air attacks; or (3) Without the maximum strength of attack of conventional ground forces, this fire would have become as large and costly as the Timber fire as a minimum and might have become as large and disastrous as the Coyote fire in Santa Barbara." (This last-named fire caused hundreds of thousands of dollars' worth of damage to residences on the inland side of Santa Barbara.) Eighty-two acres were burned in the Sisar Canyon fire and its suppression involved the work of 280 men, of which 110 were furnished by the Ventura County Fire Department. The total cost of suppression of this fire was estimated at $42,500.

This was, of course, a small fire, and was completely suppressed within a little more than twenty-four hours. An example of what can happen when a fire is hard to suppress occurred in Idaho a month before the Sisar Canyon fire in California. This was the so-called Sundance Fire, which started on private lands outside the Kaniksu National Forest protected by a local property owners' protective association. As a result of inadequate suppression efforts because of the large number of fires burning in the neighborhood, this particular fire had been contained for a week but not extinguished. Suddenly, at 10 o'clock at night on August 29, 1967, it flared up and raced downhill toward the town of Cooling, Idaho. Two days later the fire became hotter, and at 2 o'clock on the afternoon of September 1, to quote a summary issued by the Forest Service, the fire "literally blew up and raced northeast towards the Kaniksu National Forest." By 10 o'clock that evening it had burned more than 50,000 acres, and had run eighteen miles on a front averaging about four and a half miles in width, and burning a square mile of good timber every five or six minutes. Smoke from the fire rose to a height of 40,000 feet, and the heat increased the wind velocity to around 100 miles per hour. To control the fire was exceptionally difficult. More than 2,200 fire fighters were concentrated on checking it, with the help of sixty-eight bulldozers and fourteen helicopters. The cost of suppression and mopping up was estimated to be in the neighborhood of $4,000,000. When the Forest Service took over direction of fighting the fire it was able to get personnel from other branches of the Federal government. It also brought in two groups of Indians who had long had the reputation of being exceptionally good fire fighters. There have been larger areas of destruction in a single fire, but this particular one was noted for the extraordinary speed with which it moved.

Fortunately, cooperation between the U.S. Forest Service and state divisions of forestry in fighting fires is common. Details differ from state to state, but as a rule, when state or county interests are threatened by fires in or near a National Forest, or when a National Forest is endangered by fires originating on private property outside the boundaries of the National Forest but near it, cooperation in suppression becomes almost automatic. It is in the interest of all levels of government to prevent spread of fire, and they know that delay in attacking a blaze at the start increases the risk that it will get out of control.

Often when state forest lands adjoin National Forests there is what is called by the U.S. Forest Service a "red line" which parallels the boundary of the Forest, generally at a distance of a mile or more *outside* it. There is also what is called by the state a "blue line," which parallels the National Forest boundary a mile or more *inside* the Forest. Whenever a fire starts inside this mutual-aid zone, immediate steps are taken to check it by the party that spots it, without waiting for the arrival of the suppression crew of the unit that has jurisdiction. The discovery of such fire is, of course, at once reported to the unit that controls the land where the fire started, but because of the need for prompt action, and because of the interest of both parties to prevent the spread of fires anywhere near its own boundaries, immediate action can be—and almost always is—initiated by the bureau that discovers a fire within the red and blue lines. It is pertinent to note that when the members of the California Division of Forestry were explaining to me how this cooperation works, they stressed the fact that suppression of fire on ranches and other private lands is an accepted function of the State Division of Forestry with which the U.S. Forest Service gladly cooperates.

I had an enlightening confirmation of the concern of state and Federal foresters to prevent a fire from getting started on private land. Two years ago, while a strong, very dry, hot wind was blowing I was awakened at 3 A.M. by a crackling sound and bright flashes. I realized that these could only be caused by branches of a tree being blown close enough to the nearby coast power line to arc. As I live a half mile outside the Los Padres National Forest in California, and as for years the U.S. Forest Service has had an arrangement with the state of California giving the Forest Service the responsibility of fire protection in this area, I immediately telephoned the ranger station in Big Sur to report what was happening. Within fifteen minutes a suppression crew arrived. They confirmed the danger of fire and radioed the power company in Monterey, which dispatched an emergency squad—an hour's drive down the coast highway. In the meantime the rangers unloaded their fire-fighting equipment, ready to use it if a fire started before the power company's squad arrived. When the linemen came they cut back the tree that had been arcing and checked other potential danger spots. Not until all possible sources of fire had been dealt with did the rangers go back to bed. For them their mission was a routine precautionary measure. The fact that my property lies outside the boundary of the Los Padres National Forest in no way deterred them from their concern. The reason is the obvious one—that in the fire season rangers are as anxious to prevent the start of fires outside their forests, but near them, as they are to check fires within the forest bounds.

I emphasize this because it dramatizes the role of the Forest Service in this all-important field of fighting forest fires. Only fire is more destructive of natural and scenic resources than are the practices of many of the lumbermen, real-estate operators, and strip miners. So long as these men destroy only their own land they cannot be challenged or enjoined. But because fire is all consuming, it follows that effective fighting against forest fires is a direct attack on the greatest enemy of conservation. In fact, it may be said that the fire-fighting activities of the U.S. Forest Service give the service the place of honor as the leader in the practical preservation of vast areas of what remains of the nation's natural resources.

UNCLE SAM, LANDLORD

No GOVERNMENT bureau in the United States administers such a vast empire as does the Bureau of Land Management (BLM) in the Department of the Interior. Its holdings (including most of Alaska) approximate 457,000,000 acres. In what used to be termed the "Continental United States" (i.e., the old forty-eight states), BLM still has just under 176,-000,000 acres. This compares with approximately 165,600,000 acres in the same area administered by the U.S. Forest Service. In Alaska BLM has about fourteen acres for each one acre under the U.S. Forest Service.

Obviously BLM's landholdings are potentially of interest to conservationists. It is therefore heartening to read in the bureau's publications that it "is broadly concerned with the survey, engineering, inventory, classification, evaluation, administration, development, improvement, conservation and multiple use of public lands and natural resources," and to learn that its responsibilities include soil protection and erosion reduction, the management of water resources, the administration of mining law, the multiple use of timber lands, and the management of recreation resources.

In another pamphlet BLM states that it has been guided by a set of broad goals, which it summarizes as follows:

> To manage the nation's public lands and resources wisely, to prevent waste and destructive exploitation, and to preserve and protect the priceless heritage and destiny of the public resources in the Bureau's trust.
>
> To assure the continual role of the public domain as a national storehouse of land and resources from which future national needs can be supplied as lands are dedicated to their highest use.
>
> To rebuild and restore the productivity of millions of acres whose life-giving topsoil and nourishing vegetation have been taken away by the ravages of flood, wind, fire and overuse.
>
> To harvest the products of renewable resources under sustained yield, assuring future generations of equal or better supplies.
>
> To facilitate the extraction of nonrenewable resources under conditions to prevent waste and take adequate account of future needs.
>
> To serve the entire nation by managing these lands and resources under the highest standards of competency and efficiency, and the guiding force of the national interest."

Particularly interesting about these goals and procedures is that they have been adopted by a bureau that traces its origins to the General Land Office founded in 1812, which had a long history of no concern with, or interest in, conservation. Its main duty for more than a century was to record the sales of public lands under the impetus of the westward movement of the frontier. As most of this operation was before the development of the Civil Service, the Land Office was long staffed by political appointees chosen not for competence but to pay political debts.

BLM did not acquire its new label and extended functions until 1946, when the General Land Office and the so-called Grazing Service were combined in a new agency with its new name in the Department of the Interior. Today BLM manages just under nine-tenths of the public lands under the jurisdiction of the Department of the Interior. The uses to which BLM puts these lands include grazing, timber and mineral production, watershed and game protection, and outdoor recreation—and it does a good job.

The functions of BLM were further amplified by three acts of Congress in 1964. The first, known as the Classification and Multiple Use Act, provides for the retention of parts of the public domain and the disposal of the remainder. The Public Sales Act details the manner in which Federal lands may be turned over to private individuals and to local governments. The third created the Public Land Law Review Commission to review land laws of all levels of government and to make recommendations to Congress concerning them.

There is no need to detail here the work of the BLM. But it is interesting to see that the bureau's underlying philosophy is a continuation into the late twentieth century of the concepts of conservation proclaimed by Gifford Pinchot and held by Secretary of the Interior James R. Garfield in the early 1900s—that the function of conservation is to use every part of the public lands and their resources so that they will be of most value to the largest number of people. The extent to which the views of these two men differed from ours today may be seen in the statement by Samuel P. Hays, in his excellent and well-documented volume entitled *Conservation and the Gospel of Efficiency,* that Pinchot and Garfield "believed that national parks in general should be opened for such resource development as grazing and lumbering," a proposal which strikes modern conservationists as heresy.

Today BLM, with outdoor recreation as one of the major uses of its lands, is fully aware of the value of scenery as a backdrop and setting for many recreational activities. As administrator of vast areas in the Western states that are rich in scenery, BLM realizes its opportunities as well as its obligations. As a matter of fact the mere size of BLM's empire is hard for most Americans to grasp. Nine tenths of the state of Nevada is in Federal ownership (mostly BLM). Approximately two thirds of Utah and Idaho are still owned by the Federal government, with BLM having the major share. In Wyoming and Oregon almost half the land is Federally owned, with BLM having a large slice. Even more surprising is that a little less than half the land in California is still Federally owned, of which about two thirds are in National Forests and National Parks, and most of the rest under BLM.

Much of the BLM land in California, as elsewhere in the mountain states, is relatively arid. Although some of it serves as range land and to protect watersheds, most of it has little value for agriculture. But each year whole sections are being used more and more for recreation, and BLM is steadily increasing the availability—and accessibility—of portions which are especially suited to various types of recreation. In the process it is likely to discover unsuspected recreation potentials.

The mere fact that BLM's empire is so vast—and yet so lacking in economically profitable natural resources like forests, pasture, and mines—has naturally directed the thinking of its executives toward recreational areas, of which it has many. This leads to the question: "Areas for what kind of recreation?"

After reading many books and reports on recreation—and serving for six years as a member of the California State Recreation Commission—I find the only constructive answer to this question to be: "Areas for rural recreation." Metropolitan parks and playgrounds are, of course, of utmost importance, but they are restricted by space and size, accessibility, and definite limitations as to numbers of users and hours of use, none of which bear any relation to conservation. Nonurban or rural recreation areas, in contrast, are less accessible, and for this reason likely to be less crowded, and because of their distance from town, larger and more likely to retain rural characteristics. They are of major importance in conservation because they furnish the background for the contacts of millions of Americans with the remnants of rural America.

For large numbers of users one of the major attractions of areas of this sort is that they seem like country in contrast to municipal parks. Furthermore, where municipal parks are hemmed in by concrete, nonurban parks are usually surrounded by pleasant landscape and open space. I stress these obvious differences not only because of appearance and utility but also because in urban parks the combination of accessibility and rivalry for use has resulted in greater attention being paid to games, whereas in nonurban areas agreeable surroundings enhance the enjoyment of many kinds of outdoor activities. Extensive surveys of the variety of these activities made by the Bureau of Outdoor Recreation include outdoor games and sports, but they formed only 14 per cent of the recreationists' activities in 1965, whereas walking for pleasure, driving for pleasure, and swimming accounted for nearly half the user-participation in outdoor activities. There can be little doubt that the pleasure from walking and driving derives largely from pleasant surroundings.

There are, of course, exceptions to this preoccupation with the setting—types of recreation such as motorcycling, in which the main interest is not in terrain that has visual appeal, but rather in terrain that presents a challenge to the motorcyclist's agility and recklessness. The fact that nine out of ten other visitors who have motored to recreation areas are outraged by the noise and selfish indifference of motorcyclists does not mean that motorcyclists should be excluded from parks and recreation areas. But it does mean that they should be restricted to specified areas on the simple and convincing principle that they do not have the right to spoil the vacations of persons who have come by other means of locomotion. There should be trails and areas for motorcyclists from which pedestrians and riders are excluded, and hiking and riding trails on which no motorcyclists should be permitted. There is a good precedent for this sort of zoning in the separation of activities on lakes, designating certain areas for water-skiing alone, with no swimming permitted, and others for swimming or fishing, with no motorboating or water-skiing allowed.

One of BLM's major headaches is access to parts of its widely scattered landholdings. Inside of, and adjacent to, many areas of BLM land useful for recreation are private landholdings, some dating back for decades. If BLM wishes to open an area which it controls, and the best, or perhaps the only, access is over part of a private landholding, there is nothing that the bureau can do if the owner is unwilling to grant a right of way. This is particularly troublesome in the interior of southern California, where BLM controls a large area of desert, much of this within easy reach of heavily populated southern California. Because of its lack of water it has never been used for homesteading, but it has been attracting visitors in steadily increasing numbers. For decades deserts were looked upon as wastelands, inhospitable, forbidding, unpleasant. By tradition persons entered deserts at their peril, and the sooner they left them the better. But today millions of people not only are fascinated by deserts, but plan to visit more of the arid portions of the Southwest. It has been my good fortune to ride or drive extensively through Arizona during the last sixty years, and through parts of New Mexico and much of California for a shorter time. Even in old age I have loved it as much as cruising in the isles of Greece or along the Dalmatian Coast—loved it because of the stark beauty of the land forms, the richness of the colors, and the clarity and purity of the air.

Most of BLM's deserts are near large population centers, yet because of their scarce rainfall and lack of streams the land is valueless for agriculture and grazing, and costly to subdivide. But its recreation potentials are immense—as is the demand to have access to them. Speaking before the Commonwealth Club of San Francisco in April 1968, Mr. J. R. Penny, director of the BLM in California, remarked that the present demand for recreation facilities on public domain lands exceeded the supply by nearly 800 per cent and that the demand for facilities by 1980 is expected to exceed supply by 2,400 per cent. A few months later a bulletin published by BLM reported that desert recreationists were spending nearly five million visitor days in the California desert each year, about half of them traveling more than 150 miles to reach the desert, and more than half of them staying for two days or longer. Many sought the desert to camp in solitude.

I have talked with conservationists who tend to belittle the importance of recreation. This strikes me as a narrow reaction based on an understandable—though perhaps slightly snobbish—view. But for literally millions of Americans, outdoor recreation offers the best means of enjoying the fruits of conservation, from which the conclusion is obvious that recreation resources are as valuable as are timber or mineral resources. I confess to finding it hard to understand locking up spectacular areas so that no one can see them, as the wilderness lovers want. If this sort of exclusion could prevent the physical destruction and consumption of choice portions of our scenic heritage, a reasonable argument could be made for it. But the truth is that the pressing need is not so much to keep visitors out of wilderness areas as it is to save areas of outstanding natural beauty from physical mutilation by all kinds of consumers of natural resources, including road builders and builders of dams. Most of the damage done to scenic resources is not done by travelers and vacationists, but rather by commercial and other consumers of natural resources.

Fortunately most outdoor recreationists do not injure or consume natural resources unless and until a particular site becomes seriously overcrowded. Then the possible damages to the scenic resources from excessive overcrowding can be avoided by restricting the number of visitors to a definitely controllable maximum.

One of the many good points about BLM is that it is aware of the need for bureaus of governments of different levels to work cooperatively in kindred fields and to establish and maintain reasonably frequent contact. I have seen enough of bureaucracies of different levels to know that whether a bureau does its work well or poorly it guards its prerogatives jealously and takes special pains not to overstep its bounds or yield to any other bureau any of the powers which it has always exercised by itself. From talks with various BLM executives, and from my knowledge of the friendly relations that have for years persisted between the BLM and the California Resources Agency, I am satisfied that the BLM is performing a difficult custodial job with efficiency and thoughtfulness. Only a portion of its work has to do with the conservation of resources or the provision of recreation facilities, but this work is being diligently carried out, with a broad awareness of the importance of cooperation with other bureaus of other governments, including state and county units.

10

WANTED: REGIONAL PARKS

THE establishment of the Outdoor Recreation Resources Review Commission (ORRRC) in 1958 and the creation of the Bureau of Outdoor Recreation (BOR) by congressional act in 1963 stand out as two major events in the history of conservation. I suggest that the most important word in both titles is "outdoor." What counts is not the *form* of recreational activity but *where* it is enjoyed. For many Americans recreational activity is a good excuse for "getting back to nature," which shows what changes have come about since the westward trek ended with the passing of the frontier. Settlers a century ago sought soil, not scenery.

I do not know in whose fertile mind ORRRC was conceived, but I suspect that Laurance S. Rockefeller and W.H. Whyte had much to do with it. The reports by the groups set up under the auspices of the Outdoor Recreation Resources Review Commission will long help and encourage the salvaging of unspoiled remnants of our scenic heritage and will continue to inspire further land acquisition.

The value of the overall survey contained in the many volumes of the ORRRC reports is that the material is helping to clarify the thinking of persons concerned with conservation and regional planning. Basic in the ORRRC reports is the fact that in 1960 two out of three Americans were living in metropolitan areas and that this proportion will increase to three out of four by the end of the century. During this same time the land space consumed for urban uses will double, as will population, and the overall demand for outdoor recreation will triple. The reports point out that adequate provision was not being made for the rapidly expanding recreational needs of the American people, who are seeking the outdoors as never before, and that the recreation problem is not one of *numbers* of acres, but of *effective* acres. They list six classes of recreation areas: (1) high density; (2) general outdoors; (3) natural environment; (4) unique natural; (5) primitive; (6) historic and cultural. The overall goal is summarized in the statement that "the greatest possible variety of outdoor recreational opportunities and values should be available to every citizen."

BOR came into existence at the suggestion of ORRRC. One of its major contributions is that it helps in the acquisition of land for parks and recreation areas where these are most needed—in the counties and rural regions within easy reach of population centers and also in the cities themselves. BOR is doing this in the face of fierce rivalry for land for industrial, real-estate, and other developments, and is doing it at a time when land prices have reached exorbitant heights and seem sure to continue to soar. The bureau's most important contribution is in counseling, encouraging, and helping the states financially. It is a planning, coordinating, and policy-forming agency, and has no land-management functions.

Basic in its planning is the recognition of the great need for recreational opportunities near large concentrations of population.

The organization act of the BOR starts with the declaration that it is desirable that all the American people of the present and future generations "be assured adequate outdoor recreation resources and that it is desirable for all levels of government and private interests to take prompt and coordinate action . . . to conserve, develop and utilize such resources for the benefit and enjoyment of the people." Among its functions is planning to protect the natural beauty of the environment and to see that recreation resources are set aside in various parts of the country. A booklet published by BOR refers to the bureau's duty to "prepare and maintain a continuing inventory and evaluation of the nation's outdoor recreation needs and resources," and to "administer a program of financial assistance to the states, and through states to local public agencies for planning, acquiring and developing public outdoor recreation resources."

Speaking before a House subcommittee on National Parks and Recreation on April 21, 1969, Mr. Lawrence N. Stevens, then acting director of BOR, described the need of focusing attention on "people and leisure time in relation to resources use," and said that foremost among the bureau's objectives is the preservation of environmental quality. He made a particular point of stressing the fact that the Bureau is not a land managing agency, and described it as being, instead, "a policy, planning, technical assistance, research and coordinating agency," and emphasized that the Bureau's main concern is to provide recreation activities for people where they live—which implies that one of the Bureau's main functions is to help promote the establishment of recreation areas in metropolitan districts.

The effectiveness of BOR was greatly strengthened by the passage of the "Land and Water Conservation Fund Act" in 1965. This Act made available approximately $100,000,000 each year. Of the total appropriated up to and through 1968 about 27 per cent was allocated for assistance to the National Park Service, about 13 per cent to the Forest Service, and one per cent to the Bureau of Sport Fisheries and Wildlife. The remainder was allocated to the fifty states and their political subdivisions.

In discussing the operations of the Land and Water Conservation Fund, Mr. Stevens noted that the funds made available to the National Park Service and U.S. Forest Service are used primarily for buying up "inholdings." He pointed out that the purpose of granting funds to states on a matching basis is to stimulate state activity and to encourage states to take the lead in fulfilling the recreation needs of their people. Under the terms of the Act, 40 per cent of the allotments to the states is divided equally among all states; 20 per cent is apportioned on the basis of a state's total population; another 20 per cent on the basis of its urban population. The remainder depends on minor differences.

It is clear from Mr. Stevens's testimony before the House Committee that the relations between the bureau and the states are still open to differences of opinion. This was inevitable in the light of the fact that the bureau deals with fifty state governments and that the needs and attitudes of the states differ. One of the surprising differences of opinion had its origin in the fact that a number of states wanted to be able to use funds for development whereas the bureau felt that a high percentage of the grants should be for the acquisition of land. The states' attitude seems unusual in a period when supplies of land are diminishing and prices skyrocketing.

It is significant that the Act provides help to the States, counties and cities in acquiring land, but does not authorize BOR to provide funds for operation and maintenance. Every project requires BOR approval before Federal funds can be allocated for it. This insures experienced and disinterested review of each project.

A release by BOR summarizing the Land and Water Conservation Fund program further specifies that under this program prime importance is attached to: "(1) development of basic rather than elaborate facilities; (2) projects which will serve large numbers of people; (3) development of active over passive facilities; (4) acquisition in and near urban areas; and (5) projects furnishing a broad range of outdoor recreation uses and experiences. All projects must be sponsored by a public agency and open to, and primarily for, the general public."

Excellent as are the provisions of the Land and Water Conservation Fund Act there are signs that the usefulness of the Act may be nullified by inadequate financing. This is in no sense a fault of those who drafted the Act or who administer it, but rather is traceable to the competition for Federal funds which, in turn, is affected by major national and international needs, and by the unavoidable pressures of partisan politics. With the unforeseeable—and unavoidable— need for more money in the international struggle over southeast Asia, and with the equally unavoidable need for huge sums for the improvement of living conditions in most urbanized areas, together with the possible implications of steadily worsening race relations throughout the nation, the cause of conservation will be lucky if it continues to be permitted to pick up financial crumbs. The United States Treasury is not a bottomless pit. But the total annual appropriations for the BOR form only a fraction of 1 per cent of the total Federal budget, and when Congressmen get bitten by an economy bug they start by thumbing through the Federal budget and deleting all the small items that lack strong political support. As the amount requested for the Land and Water Conservation Fund payments for the fiscal year 1969 and 1970 was in the neighborhood of $100,000,000 dollars, where other appropriations run in billions, congressional blue pencils are likely to be sharpened when the next budget comes up for consideration and to be used to cut appropriations for conservation.

It is BOR's good fortune that by special act of Congress in 1968 it was provided that the Land and Water Conservation Fund would receive either from the general fund in the Treasury, or portions of the outer continental shelf, mineral-leasing receipts, as needed to insure the Land and Water Conservation Fund $200,000,000 a year for five fiscal years ending in 1973, to facilitate the acquisition of lands before prices become unduly high. But this, also, can be cut or eliminated by new legislation.

Even if the pessimists are right and the hoped-for large grants are not made, BOR can continue important service in connection with planning and coordination. Like the National Park Service and the U.S. Forest Service, BOR is staffed by experienced men with a high sense of public duty. They are happily free from the tendency which seems so often to be in evidence in long-established bureaucracies—to be more concerned with what *not* to do than with constructive achievements. I am sure that BOR has ahead of it a long and fruitful career, not only in coordinating and encouraging relations between the Federal and state governments, but also in coordinating the work of the numerous bureaus of the Federal government which, in different departments, are concerned with problems of conservation.

As this volume goes to press, signs multiply that additional cuts in the appropriations for the work of BOR are imminent. If such cuts are made they will injure the cause of conservation where it most needs help—facilitating the establishment of regional and local parks and recreation areas near large population centers. The weakness in the traditional method of carving National Parks, Monuments, and Forests out of lands already in Federal ownership is, as I have shown in earlier chapters, that most of the Federally owned lands were—and still are—in the relatively scantily populated portions of the Western states and Alaska, which means that the only way to acquire lands for parks and recreation areas in most of the states from the Rockies east to the Atlantic was—and still is—by purchase or gift. BOR was hailed by thoughtful conservationists largely because it provided political machinery for giving practical assistance to states to increase the areas of state, county, and local recreation sites throughout the entire country.

The importance of non-Federal parks and recreation areas is made plain in the next four chapters, which deal with the activities of four different states in this field. None is exclusively dependent on Federal funds—far from it. But as most states are pressed by urgent demands for state funds for all kinds of uses, and as conservation in so many states is regarded as hardly worthy of the attention of practical men, the share of appropriations available at the state level for conservation purposes is likely to be small, and to be made available reluctantly.

Fortunately BOR can continue to do valuable work in coordinating information about recreation activities of all levels of government. But it is to be hoped that instead of restricting appropriations for the Land and Water Conservation Fund which BOR administers, these can be substantially increased. After all, these are not expenditures but investments. The bulk of appropriations to this fund will be used for the acquisition of land for public use through the states. Curtailment of these funds will surely result in the loss of many areas which could and should be saved.

11

OREGON CAPITALIZES SCENERY

OREGON has been described as "essentially an outdoor state." Its urban areas are small. The western third of the state remains heavily forested as far inland as the eastern half of the spectacular Cascade Mountains. One of the three largest American rivers draining into the Pacific—the Columbia—has gouged out a huge gorge that forms part of the state's northern boundary. Shorter rivers farther south have cut through the Coast Range to the sea. The state's two hundred and fifty miles of broad, clear beaches shelve slowly and sedately into the ocean, much of which is shallow near shore, occasionally broken by rocky headlands.

Oregon's unique position in the conservation movement is due not alone to its scenic resources but also, and perhaps even more, to the fact that for decades leading Oregonians have been proud of their scenic heritage and eager to save much of it for posterity. Pioneering has, of course, left scars, but as one of the old-timers put it, early Oregonians had to "ax" their way from the Cascades to the coast. Without clearing trees they could not plow or plant. Yet because more than half of the state's area is still under Federal jurisdiction, fine stands of virgin timber remain under the protection of the U. S. Forest Service and the Bureau of Land Management. The fact that they are in Federal custody does not, *ipso facto,* mean that all of them will be saved forever from selective cutting. But when the Forest Service sells timber it designates the trees to be cut and keeps tab on the cutter. If a good part of Oregon's virgin timber had not been included in National Forests in the early days of the U. S. Forest Service, these lands would have been open to acquisition by the lumber interests which, traditionally, have been destructive in their methods of harvesting timber. In other words, Oregon owes a part, at least, of its present magnificence to the fact that segments of its forests were included in National Forests in the days of Theodore Roosevelt and Gifford Pinchot.

But of even greater importance is the fact that the state government's policy inaugurated a half century ago linked the acquisition of parks and recreation areas with the development of roads and placed both functions under the control of the State Highway Commission. This policy differed from the practices of the other states, and thanks to the Oregon Highway Commission's early acquisition of lands for parks and recreation before land prices became exorbitant, many areas near state highways were bought so as to enable motorists to stop and enjoy the scenery.

When thus described the concept of combining highways and parks seems so sound as to need no elaboration. Yet the linking of the two functions still strikes highway engineers in other states as unrealistic, despite the fact that the combination rests on the sound premise that even though many roads were built primarily for trucking, they carry large and steadily growing numbers of passenger cars. Much of this traffic consists of tourists—to such an extent that by 1967 Oregon listed expenditures by vacationists as ranking third in the relative importance of the state's sources of income. The Oregon Highway Commission even went so far as to base its policy on the sound, but then unusual, assumption that much of the pleasure derived from driving depends on agreeable surroundings. Few Americans in the 1920s gave much thought to roadside scenery. For them roads were merely links in the nation's transportation system. But Oregon's businessmen and politicians believed that scenery could be capitalized not only in the laying out of roads, but also in their use. Cynics have hinted that Oregon's awareness of scenery was hardly conscious, but rather was a by-product of the fact that Oregon had so much scenery it was hard to avoid saving some of it. Yet the logic of the state's policy was sound—that roads could and should be pleasant for traveling as well as useful for trucking timber and other commodities. The two functions were not incompatible even though recent development of scenic roads in various parts of the nation suggests that a trend toward the separation of the two types of traffic may become possible or desirable.

Oregon's concern about tourists early led to another new concept: that travelers on highways like to be able to stop—some to photograph, others to picnic, still others to rest and enjoy the scenery. Furthermore, an increasing number want to camp overnight because of the high cost of rented rooms in villages and towns. By furnishing these facilities the state accepted the fact that enjoyment was a normal by-product of travel and therefore deserved consideration by road planners. As a result the Oregon Highway Commission sought to acquire lands near to, or conspicuous from, highways if their preservation would enhance public enjoyment of the drive.

Of special interest was the fact that Oregon's early legislation establishing the responsibility of the commission for the acquisition and maintenance of parks and recreation areas was specific and constructive. It directed the State Highway Commission—I quote—"to acquire by purchase, agreement, gift, or by exercise of the powers of eminent domain ground necessary for the culture of trees and for the preservation of lands and other objects of attraction and value adjacent to, along or in close proximity to state highways." It went on to explain that the Highway Commission was authorized to "acquire land which might be necessary for the development and maintenance of parks, parking places, auto campsites, recreation grounds and resorts which, in the opinion of the State Highway Commission, are necessary for the convenience of the public and which are so situated as to be accessible from the highway." The law specified that such places should "afford the traveling public necessary conveniences and accommodations and suggested in connection with the use of public highways that these may be preserved and made available for public use, including representative stands of virgin timber and other scenic areas valuable for recreational use which are advantageously located along public highways."

So novel was this concept that we may well ask: "How come?"

The answer is twofold. First, Oregon was unusually fortunate that the State Highway Commission was—and remains—manned by public-spirited citizens of exceptionally high character. Few such bodies—and it should be noted that the members of the commission are not paid for their work—have consistently been so effective in their public service. Secondly, just as the U. S. Forest Service was lucky to have had Gifford

Pinchot to start it on its long course of useful work, and just as the National Park Service had Stephen T. Mather and his competent successors to guide that bureau's growth, so the state of Oregon had the right man in the right place at the right time. This was Samuel H. Boardman who, three years after the legislation was enacted, became in 1929 Oregon's first park superintendent. Those who knew him—he died in 1953—speak of him with affection and admiration. One who worked closely with him in the search for areas between Oregon's Coast Highway and the State's magnificent beaches to be set aside to be used by passing motorists, told me that Sam Boardman often spoke of these spots as his "jewels." He chose the finest bits, which meant that, like all good collectors, he not only had to know what to buy but had also to be able to pay for it. This meant that he had first to find a "jewel," then induce the owner to sell, and finally get the state to supply the money to buy, which, for a state employee, is often hard to do. Boardman's keen eye often spotted key sites which his superiors hesitated to purchase "sight unseen." I was told that when he had a chance to snap up a "jewel" for a song, and his superiors hesitated or refused to authorize the funds, he would find some wealthy Oregonian to buy the land as a gift to the state.

I never met Boardman, which I regret, as I am sure from what I have heard and read about him that he was one of the "greats" in the American conservation movement. But I have a copy of an editorial from the *Portland Oregonian* which describes him as a "great-framed white-haired man who occasionally gives the impression of looking like a kindly polar bear in a long overcoat." It seems clear that he was a dreamer as well as a doer, but that his dreams were practical rather than visionary. When he homesteaded in a dry part of eastern

Oregon long before he became superintendent of parks, it irked him that this region was treeless. So he planted trees, not only on his own land but, with the aid of the school children, on the school grounds and along the nearby highway. On this stretch of road he ringed his transplants with cactus. When someone asked him why he planted cactus, he explained tartly: "I am strictly averse to having rabbits girdle my trees in any manner, but I'll be damned if I am going to let them sit down to do it." The editorial in the *Oregonian* included two illuminating sidelights. One summed up Boardman's own idea of his job of buying lands for state parks: "Let's get the land while it is still available before the price goes out of reach." The other was a comment by the editor that "Retention of the natural ruggedness was perhaps the key to Boardman's philosophy of park development, and that this should be done, if possible, without felling a tree, moving a rock, or cutting a shrub." This same editorial unintentionally throws a light on Boardman's many difficulties in getting money for parks by stating that in the period from 1917 to 1953, which includes Boardman's service as park superintendent, the state spent for the acquisition and development of parks slightly less than two thirds of 1 per cent of the amount spent for highway construction. In other words, for every dollar which Boardman spent on parks the engineers spent more than a hundred dollars on roads, which, I suspect, lends even greater distinction to what Boardman actually achieved. One of his associates, Merle Chessman, who had been a member of the State Highway Commission and also a state senator, is quoted as having said: "When Sam gets out on the trail of a park he'll get it if it takes twenty years." Chessman added that "Sam had saved the state of Oregon millions of dollars in park acquisition costs by his policy of getting a park by the best means at hand whether state money was available or not." Boardman obviously had what Chessman called "a long-term persuasiveness which rarely failed him."

What Oregon has done shows that the traditional separation between state highway departments and administrators of parks and recreation areas in most other states is hard to justify. Many miles of highways have been built primarily for commercial traffic. But the need for protection in areas of outstanding scenic beauty has become increasingly important, and today is greater than ever if we are to forestall and prevent destruction of the relatively little that remains of our rapidly dwindling scenic resources by would-be exploiters.

Another aspect of Oregon's policy of linking parks with highways impressed me as I was being driven by the highway department's landscape engineer, Mr. Mark Astrup, up the Umpqua River valley which cuts through the coast range from east to west. Much of the road follows the southern bank of the Umpqua at varying distances from the river. In this strip were occasional landholdings, most of which looked more like hunting or vacation camps than permanent residences. Mr. Astrup pointed out that the state was acquiring as much of this area as possible to add to the highway right of way, with the hope and expectation that the highway department would end up owning most of the land between the road and the south bank of the river. Even more significant was the fact that at a number of bends in the river where, as we drove eastward, we had fine views of the crest of the gorge several hundred feet above us, the Highway Commission was negotiating to buy substantial parcels of land, some as much as forty acres, for the express purpose of insuring that the present views from the highway would remain unspoiled.

He explained that the highway department is seeking to obtain the cooperation of other public agencies in protecting and maintaining the natural scenic values of this route. The department already has an agreement with the county, that the county's holdings will be preserved for recreational uses. The department also is negotiating with the State Forestry Division, which has considerable holdings in and near the southern crest of the gorge, and also with the Federal Bureau of Land Management and the U.S. Forest Service, which have land on the north bank of the river. The department's objective is to see that there shall be what Mr. Astrup called a "scenic corridor," which is substantially larger than a scenic strip, alongside the right of way. He showed me a map indicating precisely what parcels of land the highway department hoped to include. I was interested to note that besides the department's action to preserve county and state forest lands, the U.S. Forest Service has designated their large holdings as a "landscape management area." What seems significant about this particular project is that it is a practical illustration of the benefits deriving from combining highways and state parks and recreation areas in a single department.

The drive up the Umpqua valley is superb, but the gorge is not of such a nature as to warrant its inclusion in a state or a national park, even if money were available to do so. Yet the sure preservation of the broad corridor through which this highway passes was accepted as a desirable ideal and its implementation was left to the department's landscape engineer, who has long had an active part in the acquisition and development of many of Oregon's state park and recreation areas. In a sense the details of what he sought to accomplish concern us less than does the fact that the state of Oregon is so wedded to the close interrelationship between saving scenery and the enjoyment of driving through it that it is following a broad-gauge program such as few, if any, state highway divisions have considered. It is interesting to note that the U.S. Forest Service, which holds tracts of virgin timber bordering on a number of state highways, has given assurances that a substantial strip of primeval forest will be left along the highway right of way so that in the possible event that some of the forest behind these strips might ultimately be made available for cutting, they would be hidden from the roadside by the screen of virgin timber.

In dealing with the billboard problem Oregon also has based its policy on the protection of scenery. One approach has been through use of the device of so-called "scenic areas." The law defines a scenic area as "an area adjacent to or along a segment of a public highway that is within a Federal or State park, is a site of historic significance, or affords a view of natural beauty that has been established as a scenic area by the scenic area commission." (The scenic area commission is a body created to evaluate such scenic areas.) It is true that this definition, as Mr. Astrup has pointed out, in practice has "eliminated pleasant pastoral views and disqualified sections east of the coast highway from scenic classification." Nevertheless 2,833 miles have been so designated. All signs are to be removed within seven years of the commission's action except those technically known as "on premise" signs. A state-wide survey has been made of tracts of land adjacent to highway rights of way, having special landscape values, as the first logical step in a continuing acquisition program. Among the features of primary importance to the natural beauties of highways he listed tracts of forest lands, woodlands or groves of trees, stream, lake, or ocean areas, mountain lookouts and turnout points, potential spring development areas, and points of unusual geological or historic interest. Speaking in terms of procedure, he stated that from the standpoint of preservation and development of scenic strips outright acquisition of such strips by purchase seems obligatory, but he also pointed out that for less significant areas, including pasture lands, scenic easements might furnish an appropriate means of control. It is encouraging to note that in the Oregon legislation regulating the establishment of billboards along interstate highways, the provision has been written that no commercial signboard can be erected within two thousand feet of another signboard on the same side of the road. Here again what strikes the outsider as so interesting is not so much the effectiveness of the attack, but rather that scenery and natural beauty are accepted as distinct and powerful influences in the thinking and planning of Oregon's road builders.

Another example of this same kind of approach is to be found in the so-called Willamette River Park System or Greenway. The Willamette flows from south to north, and joins the Columbia River at Portland. The valley comprises about a tenth of the state's area, but holds about three quarters of the state's population. It contains about two thirds of Oregon's industries and a sixth of its agriculture. The river is broad and deep and in its early days was served by large river steamboats. In appearance much of the river has been described as essentially a tree-lined corridor which winds and threads its way from Eugene, in the middle of the state, to Portland in the north. The proposed Greenway would include river access facilities such as boat launching ramps, as well as beaches, campsites, recreational trails, scenic drives, and scenic conservation areas. Because of the fact that part of the Willamette River area has been settled for over a century and because of the large proportion of Oregon's 2,000,000 population living in the valley, it is clear that a large recreational area in these surroundings will be difficult and costly to establish if the lands are not soon acquired. I have been told by persons who have canoed along stretches of the Willamette that despite the fact that the river was long used as an inland waterway and that today it traverses a relatively thickly populated area, whole stretches still give the impression of being a wilderness. One of the reasons for this is that the fall of the river between Eugene and Portland is relatively slight, with the result that even within historic times the stream has done a lot of meandering, and that it is bordered on both sides in many places by marshes or wetlands.

Although I have not been over the area I have talked with those who know it, and have read the publications of the Oregon Highway Department and other government units which are concerned in forwarding this project. Looking back on the disastrous consequences of the failure to provide long-range conservation-plus-use plans for major eastern rivers such as the Hudson, the Schuylkill, and the Potomac, the Willamette Greenway project seems intrinsically sound and still timely.

Stuart Udall, who was Secretary of the Interior from 1961 to 1969, wrote for the *National Parks Magazine* an interesting analysis of this project, in which he placed special emphasis on the importance of checking water pollution not only in the Willamette and Columbia rivers, but throughout the nation. He pointed out that within the last few decades the waters of the Willamette have become so fouled by industrial waste as to endanger not only local fishing but the run of anadromous fish. (Webster defines the word as meaning "going up river to spawn.") These include salmon, steelhead, and other salt water fish, which not only have been sharply reduced but are in danger of being completely eliminated due to the effect of pollution on the oxygen content of the water.

The objective of the Willamette Greenway has been described as "the preservation and enlargement of the river's natural environment while at the same time developing the widest possible recreational opportunities in a manner that injures no one and benefits all." Starting from the assumption that a large part of the area necessary for the project consists of marginal lands subject to varying degrees of flooding, it makes clear that local residents along the river have long been interested in river-bank preservation and wisely suggests that a program such as the Greenway should be carried out by units of local government along the river. The governor's report expressly states: "The Greenway should not be exclusively a state project." It adds that a Greenway program to be effective will require broad public support and suggests that development of such support should be a central purpose of the Greenway Committee. The report points out that the use of easements could provide for the protection of scenic qualities along the river bank where land is not needed for recreational development and still keep the lands on the tax rolls. The use of easements would permit the continuance of other compatible uses without endangering the Greenway concept.

The project will doubtless be modified when the complex difficulties of reconciling conflicting uses are worked out, together with those of implementing or reapportioning plans for active participation by units of local governments. But what stands out is that here, again, Oregon is basing a major conservation policy on the value of scenery—on what users of the Greenway will actually see. The state is saying in effect that the major objective is twofold: to protect what remains of the area for recreational uses and to insure that the end product will be agreeable to the eye. In fact, the Greenway concept may be described as an extension of the concept of scenic roads and corridors. Its objective is to save the Greenway scenic resources for long-term enjoyment.

Secretary Udall, in the article to which I have referred, points out that inasmuch as the Greenway centers on a river, the condition of the water is of major importance. This, of course, is true. Pollution can ruin or seriously damage the Greenway. But the problem of pollution will be just as severe if no such project is developed. In fact, the building of the Greenway would be another, and very important, reason why pollution of the Willamette is being checked—as pollution should be checked everywhere. The Greenway appears to be off to a good start. Its development will be watched with interest by conservationists in many parts of the country.

In Salem and Portland I heard on all sides that—at least during the last ten years—no Oregonian had done more in guiding the state's highway and park policies than has Mr. Glenn L. Jackson, who has been a member of the State Highway Commission since 1959 and has been chairman of the commission since 1962. He has been for years head of the Pacific Light and Power Company, one of the largest distributors of electric power in the Northwest.

On talking with him about the work of the Highway Commission, I asked him what the commission looked forward to accomplishing in the next few years. He said that one of its aims was to bring about closer cooperation with the Federal agencies in planning for the development and use of the recreational facilities on Federal lands within the state boundaries. He pointed out that of the little more than half of Oregon's total area still controlled by Federal government bureaus, the U. S. Forest Service, and the BLM, each has jurisdiction over about 15,000,000 acres and that other Federal agencies control a total of about 2,000,000 acres. He explained that these Federal holdings represent 90 per cent of Oregon's underdeveloped recreational possibilities, but he added:

> Our Commission is in constant touch with the U. S. Forest Service, which controls more land with recreation potentials than does any other bureau of the Federal government. We hope to obtain from the Forest Service an inventory of scenic values and recreation potentials within National Forest lands inside the state borders so that we can work with them on such matters as approach roads and can encourage tourists to visit these National Forest areas. As you know, the Forest Service is now deeply interested in the use of National Forest lands for recreation purposes, and as we are already using most of our own potential recreation areas under the state's jurisdiction, we shall have to rely more and more on the Forest Service to help accommodate the steadily increasing number of travelers.

> I suspect that most visitors to Oregon neither know nor care what recreation areas are administered by the state and which are under the care of the Forest Service, just as many persons who visit Federal lands do not distinguish between areas under the National Park Service and those under the Forest Service. Many visitors do not even know that each of these two big agencies operates with little reference to what the other is doing. Most tourists are interested primarily in seeing beautiful

country and in having comfortable quarters and good roads, regardless of what government bureau acts as caretaker. In fact, they neither know nor care if they are on state or Federal land. When they get home they are likely to retain definite impressions of what they have seen, but only vague ideas as to whether a particular spot was administered by the state or by a Federal bureau. And, after all, we here in Oregon cannot forget that even though the U. S. Forest Service has jurisdiction over millions of acres in Oregon these acres are inside the state's boundaries and are as much an essential part of Oregon as is the Willamette Valley.

12

RURAL PARKS FOR CITY PEOPLE

For years thoughtful residents of the Twin Cities in Minnesota wondered what could be done to devise and implement a long-range regional plan for land use in the seven counties that make up what is now called the Twin City Metropolitan Area of Minnesota. Not only were there rivalries between municipal and county governments, but rural residents distrusted city dwellers. As the area had been settled by Yankees, Scandinavians, and Germans, with a generous sprinkling of Scots and Irish, the tradition of rugged individualism was—and still is—strong in Minnesota. Rural residents did not like the idea that the seven metropolitan counties should work together in matters of common concern, such as the laying out of highways and the location of parks and recreation areas in a belt about an hour's easy drive from the Twin Cities. They asked pointed questions: "Who will use these parks and recreation areas? Who will pay for the land? Will such areas be taken off the county tax rolls? Who will administer them and pay for their upkeep?"

The answers led to a clearer understanding of the problems. Even if compensation for lost taxes could be devised, the country people hesitated to agree to anything which might lead to county funds being used to buy lands for parks for city people. In other words, rural Minnesotans were reacting toward city dwellers just as rural Americans have reacted elsewhere. The local people believed that if a public park was established near them, their land would be overrun by trespassers and their crops trampled underfoot. Furthermore, the rural counties did not want to establish permanent relations with neighbor counties, lest by joining in intercounty action they might feel obliged to support projects that might be unpopular at home. They clung to self-determination.

There was nothing new in the hesitation of counties to work together. Even Ramsay County, the county seat of St. Paul, and Hennepin County, the county seat of Minneapolis, had long been reluctant to cooperate. Nor was it unusual that a group of private citizens did much to help win support for the creation of plans for a metropolitan area. The Minnesotans had the precedent of the successful development of New York's Regional Plan Association, which had developed machinery for the close cooperation of adjacent counties and even of the three adjoining states of New York, New Jersey, and Connecticut. The Greater New York area had many problems in common which came from the concentration of population and activities within fifty miles of Manhattan Island. In Minnesota the area and the population were, of course, much smaller and the plans that were devised for the Metropolitan Area applied only to the seven metropolitan counties. Furthermore, these plans embodied ideas often expressed by prominent citizens of Minnesota during the previous half century. As long ago as 1919, Theodore Wirth, long-time superintendent of the nationally recognized Minneapolis Park System and father of Conrad Wirth, one-time director of the National Park Service, called attention to the need to acquire local and regional recreation and park sites within thirty to fifty miles of the Twin Cities.

In the early 1950s, a group of prominent Minneapolis business leaders formed the "Citizens League." The organization took its name from a Seattle group with a similar label. As one of the founders explained it to me, the League began with a bipartisan membership of about 3,000, with a paid professional research staff. When agreement was reached on issues to be studied with a view to presenting a report with recommendations, the technical work was left to professionals, and an action group of League members kept close tab on the drafting of the proposals.

To recite the details of the Citizens League's progress would go beyond the scope of this book. But the records of the League show that in January of 1953 one of its directors, Lloyd Hale, suggested that the League should sponsor a county park system, which eventually became a metropolitan system. While this cannot be pinpointed as the start of the Metropolitan Area Park movement, the League's support of the plan from that time on was a force in arousing political interest in it.

In 1955, a bill was passed by the Minnesota legislature which was described as being designed to meet the needs for scenic areas and for access to natural sites such as lakes and rivers. It also postulated that the growing population and the increase of leisure time would lead to increased demands for more parks and recreation facilities. Existing state and local parks would not be able to accommodate the expected visitors. The Citizens League spelled out the urgent need to

secure large tracts of land for park purposes to be preserved
in their natural state and stressed the fact that if they were
to be bought at a fair price, they would have to be bought
soon. The legislature was asked to provide for the appointment of a park-planning commission to draw plans to acquire
and develop park lands.

When I was in the Minnesota Metropolitan Area, I visited
a number of county park and recreation sites in Hennepin
County, some developed, others only recently acquired, and
a few in process of negotiation for acquisition. All of them
were within less than an hour's drive of Minneapolis, and
those that had already been developed seemed ideal for their
purpose. In that part of Minnesota there are, besides many
lakes and streams, a variety of one-time farm lands, mostly
with wood lots which, before the days of rural electrification,
were essential to mere survival in the long, cold winters. Besides adequate access from highways, the developed sites have
good parking facilities—at least for present usage—and these,
in turn, have been located near parts of the park sites, which
in many ways look like English country estates, with fine old
trees left for their shade and decorative value, rolling lands
bordering small lakes, and occasional streams. Trails lead
from parking lots to well-spaced picnic tables, some of which
are near simple outdoor grills. Good piped water is within
easy walking distance. Some of these picnic sites overlook
small lakes with good wading beaches. Others adjoin marsh-
lands which are of great value in connection with the movement of waterfowl and game birds. In general, the purpose
in acquiring new sites is threefold: to establish suitable recreation areas; to insure the permanent preservation of wetlands; and to set aside areas as permanent open space so as
to prevent uncontrolled real-estate development.

A report of the Hennepin County Park Reserve District specifies that county parks should be "of the best native recreation resources of the county and [be] located within 25 or 30 miles of the center of population. The native character of each is to be preserved, but they are also to be enjoyed by people. They must not be wholly developed for active use." The report gives as a policy a classification of county parks as follows: "County park reserves containing one thousand or more acres of predominantly native attractiveness devoted to daytime and overnight use, only partially, and devoted to nature appreciation principally. County recreation parks— containing approximately fifty to several hundred acres of naturally attractive land suitable for development of a wide variety of daytime uses and located so that the majority of county citizens will live within five miles of a county park or a large municipal park." The report distinguishes between county recreation parks and county park reserves: "The county park reserves must always retain and preserve their native areas. County recreation parks are acquired, developed and managed exclusively for recreation purposes . . . may be almost entirely developed for daytime but not overnight use, except that there must always be sufficient native area retained to impart the idea of spaciousness in the native out of doors."

Present prospects seem good that, at least in the Metropolitan Area, the Minnesota counties will cooperate in the setting aside of state and county parks and recreation centers. The legislation establishing the Hennepin County Park Reserve District stated expressly that it was the duty of the commission to effect "the acquisition, development and maintenance of large park, forest and other reservations and wildlife sanctuaries, and not the establishment of parks and playgrounds of local or neighborhood character." The commission report included the statement that the following principles "shall guide the development: 1) Not more than twenty percent of county park reserves shall be developed for active use: picnicking, water activities, daytime and overnight camping, trails and uses incidental thereto. The remaining eighty percent shall be retained in its natural state except where reforestation, drainage or impounding or other rehabilitation measures are taken to enhance the original native attractiveness." It adds that these native areas may be "invaded by hiking and bridle trails, and even bicycle trails, all properly controlled, but not by motorized vehicles except that pleasure driving may be established in large park reserves." The conclusion seems inescapable that at the county level broad policies with long-range objectives are now being developed and applied.

Still undetermined at the time of my visit to the Minnesota Metropolitan Area was how the acquisition and development of desired park lands beyond Hennepin County were to be financed. In 1968 a project was under continuing study to obtain a regular source of revenue which could be turned over to the counties for the purchase of additional park and recreation sites. The device which seemed to have the greatest promise when I discussed this aspect of the overall problem with friends in the Twin Cities was an increase of two cents in the cigarette tax. Nonsmokers would agree that the device is shrewd and could furnish a substantial revenue for the acquisition of park and recreation lands. But no one with whom I talked ventured to guess the nature and possible intensity of opposition to such a proposal, not only from the army of smokers but from the many groups seeking to channel revenue from the state to some particular project. Certainly the use of money from this source for the purchase of land for public use is free from any charge of undue influence.

The growing emphasis on the value of open space is likely to help the cause of conservation. Open space is the antithesis of urban and suburban development of all kinds. It embraces rural lands whether or not under cultivation. Such lands may be heavily forested, or, like so much of the American countryside, long cleared and under cultivation. They may be steep and even mountainous, gently rolling, or flat farm land. Whatever their form, they are in sharp contrast to suburban areas as well as to cities and towns. In the days of the early settlers, our modern concept of open space was nonexistent. But as urbanization advanced and population increased, with the attendant expansion of roads, industries, and all the other by-products of industrialization, the supply of open space dwindled.

When conservationists first became concerned about saving open space, they thought in terms of incorporating desirable areas into parks and recreation sites through government purchase. But it soon became clear that to buy all of the open space they thought should be protected—or even a large part of it—would run into vast sums and would create formidable political problems. Of these, the most difficult to solve would be that the permanent acquisition of land for park or openspace purposes would result in these lands being removed from the county tax rolls, which, in turn, meant that counties throughout the nation would mobilize political resistance to all such attempts—and the political force of county resistance can be formidable. In fact, the effectiveness of local opposition has been one of the main reasons why conservationists sought out devices to conserve open space without removing it from private ownership, and in particular, without in any way curtailing the use of such lands for farming.

Two devices have been tried: zoning, and resort to what the legal profession terms "easements." Zoning to date has been helpful, but it has been limited in scope and of uncertain long-range effectiveness. Zoning ordinances are of local origin, which means that what one county board of supervisors may enact by way of an ordinance can be modified or abrogated by a succeeding board of supervisors. While it may be said that the longer a zoning ordinance remains unchallenged the less likelihood is there that it will be modified or overthrown, the fact remains that zoning is still in a more or less experimental state, and zoning is at best a precarious method of preserving open space.

Apparently less vulnerable is another device to which the legal profession gives the name of "scenic easements" or "conservation easements." As one who has had no legal training, I have found it hard to put into plain words the precise meaning of an easement. When I asked a lawyer friend to explain it to me, he said, somewhat testily: "It's perfectly plain. Property is held in what we call 'fee simple.' Property is nothing but a bundle of rights. The owner of property can divest himself of one or more of these rights, and on occasion can be compelled, usually for due compensation, to surrender one or more of these rights. When he does so, we term it an easement." An organ of government—such as a county, or perhaps a state park or highway or planning commission— wishing to preserve open space can agree to pay the landowner for an "easement" under the terms of which the landowner undertakes not to subdivide or in any way deface a designated portion of his land. All uses not expressly surrendered by him remain his to enjoy, but the uses which he surrenders in the easement "run with the land." Thus the community is assured that the general character and appearance of his land will remain unchanged.

Presumably it is accepted that agricultural land may continue to be farmed. As a matter of fact, most persons interested in the preservation of open space look on agricultural use of land as desirable. It is important to note that the landowner is paid for his easement.

While the amounts vary from state to state and region to region, they are rarely more than a portion of the assessed value of the land. But in cases where the percentage runs high, the government, instead of paying for the easements, has often preferred to buy the land outright. In most instances, land which is subject to such easements pays lower tax rates than land free from easements.

Because open space is gaining in legal support and because such an important approach to the overall problem as that of Minnesota's Twin City Metropolitan Area has developed, the concept deserves careful study by conservationists regardless of their particular fields of interest. I say this because so long as the goals of the open space movement are kept within bounds, and so long as some of the legal devices can be strengthened, the pursuit of open space may be of great value within the next few years.

Another point is that in addition to the need to preserve substantial areas of the countryside because of what might be called their secondary values, such as the perpetuation of wildlife and the preservation of the land from suburbanization, there is an all-important aspect of open space of which relatively little analysis has been made. This is the visual element. In the case of open space which is visible to many persons—as, for example, areas adjacent to highways and areas to be used for parks and recreation sites—what can be seen by visitors or passers-by is of primary importance.

To Americans of this last third of the twentieth century it is surprising that this concept was so slow in being accepted. When first put forward forty years ago by the distinguished landscape architect and planner, Frederick Law Olmsted, Jr., the concept of open space as we now know it was unheard of even by the few then interested in conservation. Olmsted insisted that more people would want, and be able, to spend vacation time driving with the family to favorite swimming holes, picnic grounds or spectacular sites of nature, and that these people would enjoy their vacations all the more if the roads over which they drove led through pleasant surroundings. Today the idea is widely accepted, but for twenty to thirty years after he first enunciated it, few people were aware of its importance.

The fact that driving for pleasure is largely dependent on the roadside scene needs to be emphasized in these days when so much attention has been directed to roadside beautification. Unfortunately, one of the most powerful lobbies in the nation—the billboard lobby—continues to fight this concept. Equally unfortunately, most highway engineers throughout the United States—with the outstanding exception of Oregon—take refuge in the easy excuse that their concern is safety, not scenery. The two, of course, are not incompatible, but highway engineers, operating with limited budgets, have felt that they could not afford the luxury of saving scenery.

In analyzing the value of open space, special attention should be given to the concept of scenic corridors. This term, as I explain in the previous chapter, applies to what might otherwise be called wide and pleasant rights of way along highways where the natural beauties of the countryside are carefully preserved. Such a corridor should not be rigidly standardized as to width. Instead, the width should depend on the nature of the terrain. Where used, and whatever its label—parkway, throughway, scenic highway, or any other appropriate name—the purpose of its design is that the saving of scenic resources should be guided primarily by what the passing motorist sees.

One of the many advantages of this approach to the problem is that, by implication, a scenic corridor means that the restricted area of open space is relatively narrow. From this we deduce that a good many of the arguments in favor of open space, which apply to areas that are clearly seen by countless motorists, do not necessarily need to extend beyond the line of vision. In other words, the acquisition of open space need not be a mass operation engulfing large areas of rural land. Rather should it only apply expressly to land within the line of vision as clearly seen from the highway.

In the drawing up of Minnesota's comprehensive regional plan, the formulation of the details was worked out by the Metropolitan Planning Commission, which as early as 1962 inaugurated a series of studies made in cooperation with the Minnesota Commissioner of Highways and thirteen state and local agencies. This group published several fine reports on the problems, and in 1968 its successor, the Metropolitan Council, assembled findings and recommendations in an impressive volume called *Twin Cities Area Metropolitan Development Guide*. This comprehensive and well-presented document deals with details of metropolitan planning to assure farsighted land use for the entire area. From the point of view of conservationists, the particular interest of the *Development Guide* is its constant preoccupation with the

preservation of the area's scenic resources from the uncoordinated plans of real-estate developers.

The authors of the *Guide* stressed the urgency in planning
today for the allocation and use of the Metropolitan Area's
remaining open spaces. They knew that pressures for the con-
version of open space for the needs and demands of our industrial civilization will continue to increase. Already it has resulted in rivalry for the use—or at least the control—of areas
as yet uncluttered and unspoiled by human greed. The wise
use of such rural areas has become one of the greatest problems which conservationists face today. Volumes could be
written—with the benefit of hindsight—detailing the mistakes
of land use in the last century or more. Often these mistakes
were regarded as public benefactions. They had in their defense the fact that many of them were useful and profitable
in the process of community expansion. So, for example, most
persons familiar with the Hudson River deplore the fact that
in the early days of the railroad era, a century or more ago,
the railroad builders were encouraged to build along the
river's edge. Yet the location of the rail beds, so detrimental
to property along the river, was of great value to the nation.
In the Twin Cities Metropolitan Area, most of the shoreline
of the Mississippi, the Minnesota, and the St. Croix rivers
was used unnecessarily—but often profitably—for commercial
and industrial purposes. Wise planning could and would have
saved large stretches of the shoreline for community uses.

While this account of "open-space" objectives in the *Development Guide* is reasonably specific, I am convinced that the
term "open space" means many things to many people. I have
sought in vain for a satisfactory definition. As commonly
used, it suggests what our grandparents called "a pleasant
countryside." Before World War I, there was still so much

of this that it was regarded as inexhaustible. Yet today, it is relatively scarce, and unless well protected, most of it will be devoured by real-estate developers and highway engineers, and ultimately by urban sprawl.

Those who believe in the need to save open space know that not only is the concept hard to publicize, but that it is belittled and fought by persons who hope to profit by "developing" tracts of open space themselves. Landowners are suspicious of a project which might be interpreted as infringing on their right to do what they want with their land. When faced with proposals to forestall development, these groups fall back on the glib slogan: "You can't stop progress." Most landowners are willing to sell when prices on nearby lands reach new highs. Americans lack the British and Continental European tradition that the longer land has been in the same family, the more unthinkable is the possibility of parting with any of it.

It is one of the charms—as well as handicaps—of many conservationists that they are so zealous in the pursuit of their objectives that they tend to overlook the strong tradition behind the intended land uses of their rivals in the race for space. Only too often conservationists attract publicity in behalf of the preservation of scenic resources of all kinds, but their opponents, with strong political sagacity and support, continue blandly to stress the fact that housing developments, new office buildings, and market sites, and the establishment of industrial units, will be of much greater benefit to the community than parks and recreation areas.

Back of plans are goals. Those outlined in the *Twin Cities Area Metropolitan Development Guide* throw light on this aspect of problems of conservation. The *Guide* summarizes its open space goals and stresses open space and natural resources. It describes them as not simply leftover land, but as land which serves one of five specific functions: 1) amenity and aesthetics; 2) conservation; 3) production; 4) protection; 5) recreation. In the report's definition, open space includes parks, recreation sites, lakes, and airport clear-zones. It also stresses that the Metropolitan Open Space System should include lands that can be used for two or more open-space functions, and should acquire, develop, and operate recreation facilities for Metropolitan-wide use, including even appropriate sites beyond the boundaries of the seven-county area. Special emphasis is placed on the urgency of acquiring these before the costs become prohibitive. Because of the rapidly growing interest in the use of lakes and other water resources for all kinds of recreational activities, it urges that special attention be given to finding and acquiring such areas for ultimate public enjoyment.

I have enlarged on the open-space aspect of the Minnesota Metropolitan Area project because present indications are that it may pave the way for greater use of this device for saving scenic resources. But as one who for years has seen the relentlessness—and the success—of the opponents of saving scenic resources, I feel obliged to stress the likelihood that the easement device may be successfully challenged. This does not mean that it should not be used, but rather that its use should be regarded as expedient rather than as dependable. In his excellent study of many aspects of the saving of scenic resources, *The Last Landscape,* Mr. W. H. Whyte has brought together encouraging evidences of the growing inclination of the courts to sustain the device of easements and to recognize that aesthetics may be considered as carrying weight in various matters such as zoning. The mere fact that Whyte has such an optimistic view is in itself encouraging. He has assembled instances in which legislative action has been taken, which is likely to lessen the possibility that the device of easements will be effectively challenged.

What struck me as particularly important in the Twin City Metropolitan Area plan was the fact that those who launched it started soon enough to be able to attain many of their objectives. Land suitable for parks and recreation sites was still available within the suggested hour's drive from the Twin Cities, at prices which were not exorbitant. The combination of private support for public planning and direction made it easier to overcome the traditional indifference or hostility of local political leaders to such an all-embracing plan. Fortunately, the approach has been a broad one and is not centered exclusively on parks and recreation sites. Rather does it include new highways, real-estate and industrial development. In other words, it looks toward the overall needs of the Metropolitan Area within the next two or three decades. Undoubtedly it will be whittled down, primarily under the influence of real-estate developers backed by builders and suppliers. This has been a common pattern in all such types of planning. But if as many as a quarter of the country's counties were to do as much for conservation and take as broad a view of the value of wise planning centering on the preservation of substantial areas of open space from suburban and commercial development as has Minnesota's Metropolitan Area, there would be less for conservationists to do in the remaining years of the twentieth century. To save open space in areas of low population density and unlikely pressures from subdividers and industrial developers is easy in comparison to accomplishing the saving of desirable areas where population pressure is burgeoning. Minnesota has made it plain: good plans can win good support.

13

IOWA POINTS THE WAY

MY FIRST visit to Iowa was in 1933 during the great depression. Returning thirty-five years later I was again struck with the rampant fertility of its soil and the serene maturity of its farms and small towns. My itinerary took me on dirt roads through tunnels of tall corn, as well as along broad paved highways through rolling, well-watered country dotted with wood lots made obsolescent by widespread electric power. Every few miles we passed long-settled villages with broad shaded streets that recalled New England. It is a sedate but dynamic countryside, untouched by the soil exhaustion of much of the East and free from the economic and social immaturity common in the West.

I was surprised to find that although Iowa is one of the most extensively and intensively farmed states in the Union, with nine tenths of the land under cultivation, Iowans have for years given thought to the goal of establishing a park or recreation area within thirty miles of every town in the state. Although in the other forty-nine states interest in conservation, parks, and recreation is greater in urban than in rural districts—among the "have-nots" rather than the "haves"— the plan for parks in Iowa has strong rural support. The contrast between this attitude in Iowa and the indifference, or even hostility, to parks and recreation areas in rural regions elsewhere aroused my curiosity. How did it happen that a state of farms from border to border, with little remaining forest land, has shown so much concern about parks and recreation areas?

Several persons whom I questioned about this took refuge in the inconclusive remark that the legislators, most of whom were country bred, loved the land. Another of my Iowa friends muttered cryptically: "Fish and game," and then explained that hunting game birds and fishing in Iowa's many streams have long been favorite forms of recreation for Iowans of all ages and that they want to be sure that their children and grandchildren will have the same privilege. I suggested that there would be no hunting and fishing in these parks, but he assured me that most Iowans had sentimental ties with rural Iowa and liked the thought of setting aside small areas in all of Iowa's ninety-nine counties to show the younger generation what the country looked like in the good old days.

The plausibility of this interpretation is reflected in the history of what is now called the Iowa Conservation Commission and the expansion of its functions during the last century. As early as 1857 the Iowa General Assembly passed a law establishing seasons for the taking of certain types of game—its first attempt to conserve wildlife. Five years later it imposed a season for trout and also declared the taking of trout in any way other than by hook and line to be illegal. In 1874 several persons were appointed to look after fish and game and in time were labeled the "Fish Commission," headed by Mr. B.F. Shaw. Later the name was changed to "Fish and Game Department." No state game warden was appointed until 1897. Beginning three years later nonresidents were required to obtain hunting licenses. In 1909 similar requirements were imposed on Iowans. Residents did not need to have fishing licenses before 1922. No licenses were required for persons under eighteen years of age; now everyone over sixteen has to have a license for hunting and fishing. Youngsters below this age are still free to hunt and fish without licenses, if accompanied by a licensed adult.

The State Fish and Game Commission was established in 1931. Four years later it was consolidated with the Board of Conservation (State Parks Board). The new commission was given charge of parks, recreation, and forests, and its name was changed to the "Iowa Conservation Commission." It now has seven members, each appointed for a term of six years on a staggered basis, with not more than four affiliated with the same political party. The fish-and-game unit is still supported by sales of fishing and hunting licenses as well as by contributions from the Federal government under the terms of the Dingell-Johnson Act and the Pittman-Robertson Act. These Federal funds have been particularly helpful in acquiring and developing marshland for game management.

In 1955 Iowa's general assembly enacted Chapter 111-A, commonly called the "County Conservation Law." Few states at that time had tried to interest counties to set aside parks and recreation areas. The law deserves attention not only because it brought about county participation in conservation but because it conferred broad powers on the counties. It provided that each county in Iowa could set up a county conservation board. The counties were expressly directed to "acquire, develop, maintain and make available to the inhabitants of the county, public *museums,* parks, reserves, parkways, playgrounds, recreation centers, county forests, wildlife and other conservation areas and to promote and preserve the health and general welfare of the people, to encourage the orderly development and conservation of natural resources, and to cultivate good citizenship by providing adequate programs of public recreation."

Here in a few phrases was a new approach to problems of conservation, combining logically many objectives which had been dealt with, if at all, on a "hit or miss" basis. Furthermore, it postulated that conservation transcends national and state jurisdictions, and that it is, in fact, a major concern of local government levels. The detailed objectives include almost everything from wildlife refuges to tennis courts and are remarkable because of their variety and inclusiveness.

It is probable that the novelty of county participation in this sort of activity was a reason why the program was slow in getting under way. Most of Iowa's counties had always operated on small budgets. Under the County Conservation Law the counties were authorized to levy up to one mill on the assessed valuation of all real and personal property, but the mere authorization to do so did not insure enthusiasm for the use of county taxes for such purposes.

It was at this juncture that the Federal government came to the rescue through the enactment of the "Land and Water Conservation Fund Act" of 1965, to which I refer in Chapter X. This program accelerated county conservation planning, land acquisition, and development of county recreation areas.

Recognizing the recreation need at all government levels, the Iowa Conservation Commission directed 50 per cent of the Land and Water Conservation Funds apportioned to

Iowa each fiscal year to be reapportioned to its political sub-
divisions on a county by county basis, according to the following formula: "(1) Twenty per cent will be apportioned
equally to each county. (2) Eighty per cent will be apportioned according to each county's proportionate share of the
total state population." To be available this financial assistance has to be earmarked for specific projects, the plans of
which have been worked out by local governments and approved by the state Conservation Commission.

During the first four years the use of Land and Water
Fund payments has resulted in increased interest on the part
of local governments in Iowa to become participants in the
development of county parks and recreation areas. The mere
fact that money for the acquisition of land has been made
available to the counties has eliminated the latent fear of
local residents that their county become too deeply involved
in projects which seem to some of them to be of questionable
value to the local community. The solution of this aspect of
the problem has given a substantial boost to the development
of much-needed local areas not only in the state of Iowa but
elsewhere in the nation.

The importance of this lies in the fact that in many parts
of the country local governments were unable to finance
projects of this sort and that until the new method of financing became effective most local units did not embark actively
on park and recreation projects. In other words the availability of Federal funds for the acquisition of lands at the state
and county levels has greatly strengthened the nation-wide
movement for establishing more parks and recreation areas
outside of Federal jurisdiction. It is obvious that National
Parks and Forests cannot meet the needs of the steadily growing numbers of vacationists. Only through the spread of state,

county, and other local parks can the increasing crowds be accommodated.

By the summer of 1968 the Iowa Conservation Commission had agreed on a five-year plan providing for the acquisition of about a hundred thousand acres of land for park and recreation purposes. This plan, which has been approved by state and federal agencies, is expected to compensate for the fact that Iowa has the lowest percentage of Federally owned lands of any state in the union. In other words, the only available sources of lands for park and recreation purposes in Iowa are outside of Federal jurisdiction.

Describing the purposes of this plan, Mr. E. B. Speaker, special projects coordinator of the Iowa Conservation Commission, said; "We do not propose to convert a large percentage of agricultural lands into playgrounds, but to preserve as much as possible of the rapidly disappearing wetlands, properly manage the remaining woodlands, preserve the streams and lakes in their natural state and set aside sufficient additional land to provide for cultural and recreational enrichment of the lives of our people in this and future generations."

I also discussed this five-year plan with Professor DeWitt Nelson of the Iowa State University at Ames, who had formerly been director of the California Department of Natural Resources. He stressed the particular significance of the grouping together of different conservation functions under one administrative body. In a subsequent letter he wrote me, ". . . the strength of the Iowa program appears to be in the fact that parks and recreation, fish and game, and forests and waters are all grouped under one policy-forming Commission and one Director. Consequently, planning, development and management are much better coordinated and integrated than if each were under a separate department."

It was Iowa's good fortune that its most famous citizen in the first two thirds of the twentieth century was the nationally known cartoonist, Jay N. ("Ding") Darling. A keen angler and a dedicated conservationist, his influence was great. Any measure that he backed was nearly always well supported in the Iowa legislature. Hunters and anglers respected and liked him, even when he fought for small-bag limits on game—particularly on ducks and other migratory birds.

"Ding" was a member of the State Fish and Game Commission from 1931 to 1934. During this period he impressed on his fellow members the need for orderly planning. It was largely due to his vision and leadership that the sportsmen's organizations supported the state's conservation program.

Cheerful, rather than hilarious, "Ding" was in no sense a fanatic. His cartoons were drawn with the skill of a great artist engaged in depicting the essence of contemporary problems. He sought to clarify—not to ridicule—to help people understand, rather than to divert them by clownish absurdities. He saw the world with devastating clarity and could point up in a few lines in a single cartoon the core of a complex political or social problem. His cartoons were a major attraction of the old *New York Tribune,* which syndicated them widely throughout the nation, beginning in World War I. When, later, the *Tribune* became the *Herald-Tribune* after Frank Munsey's *New York Herald* had been merged with the *Tribune,* "Ding's" cartoons remained among the most valued features of the combined newspapers and continued to be widely syndicated.

"Ding" made his home in Iowa throughout his life but was

a frequent visitor to New York. As I was an editorial writer on the old *New York Tribune,* and subsequently on the *Herald-Tribune* for about ten years, I saw "Ding" often and once spent a week with him fishing for steelhead on the Klamath River in northern California.

In an obituary notice of "Ding" I read that his two most famous cartoons were: (1) on the death of Theodore Roosevelt; and (2) on the opening of the duck-hunting season. The first, entitled "The Long, Long Trail," was drawn the day the former President died and showed the old "Rough Rider" starting off on horseback into the skies. The second, entitled "Annual Migration of the Ducks," was published on the opening day of the duck-hunting season and showed an army of duck hunters shooting at a few crippled ducks. It was a powerful plea for greater protection for wildlife, and was widely reprinted for years by conservationists.

A story is told of "Ding"—and as far as I know never denied—that when in the early days of the New Deal "Ding's" cartoons of the then new President, Franklin D. Roosevelt, were turning many people against the New Deal, FDR, eager to silence this devastating critic, decided that the only way he could muzzle "Ding" was to give him a chance to save some ducks. He invited "Ding" to the White House and asked him if he would consider becoming head of the U. S. Biological Survey—the Washington bureau charged with the protection of migratory birds. To FDR's delight and puckish satisfaction, "Ding" accepted—and, of course, had to give up cartooning so long as he held that office. After more than a year he resigned and returned to his drawing board. For years thereafter he supported the cause so dear to him: the saving of as much as possible of the rapidly disappearing scenic and wildlife resources of the North American continent.

"Ding" was eighty-six years old when he died in 1962, but still full of enthusiasm and interest. His particular absorption at the time has come to be known as the Lewis and Clark Trail Parkway—a project on which "Ding" had spent many of the last hours of his life. Familiar with the Lewis and Clark journals, as well as with much of the terrain through which they had passed, "Ding" envisaged a scenic corridor along the major portion of the route that they followed. His idea was that even though a large part of the journey had been by canoe, raft, and portages, it should be possible to identify many of the places where they stopped, and that these should be properly marked and made accessible along a sort of historic parkway.

Thanks to the interest of friends in Des Moines to whom "Ding" had outlined this scheme, a group headed by the Des Moines banker Mr. Sherry R. Fisher, formed the Darling Foundation to implement the cartoonist's dream. Not only was money raised for publicizing the idea, but the interest of Secretary of the Interior Stewart Udall was enlisted, and shortly after "Ding" died a bill was introduced in Congress creating a National Lewis and Clark Commission, which had as its designated objective to provide for identifying, marking, and preserving the route followed by Lewis and Clark, in order to advance awareness and knowledge of the far-reaching historic significance of this journey in the development of the West. A conference was held, composed of representatives from the Federal government and the interested states, and in time the active cooperation of the new Bureau of Outdoor Recreation was enlisted to help work out an all-inclusive project.

The chances are that the actual area of the right of way along the Lewis and Clark Trail Parkway will be relatively small, as the present plans call for little more than a ribbon of protected land. But as much of the country through which the explorers passed is still for the most part unchanged, a corridor of varying width will make it possible for future travelers to see much of what Lewis and Clark saw of the country. As it is to the interest of the states through which the route passes to cooperate in saving the most scenic spots, and those of special historic interest, the success of this new kind of historic parkway is likely to be followed by similar treatment of other famous routes of explorers and immigrants—notably the Santa Fe Trail.

In theory, similar treatment might be applied to other great river routes—and is, in fact, being developed along the Mississippi River in Wisconsin and elsewhere. Interesting and important as are these projects, they are more difficult to implement than is the Lewis and Clark trail, primarily because the rivers early became heavily industrialized, with the result that the widening of existing roads or building of new ones presents serious complications, both legal and aesthetic. Wisconsin already has done much on its portion of the River Road, and Iowa has under discussion various useful projects along the river.

As I look back over my samplings of state and local projects, the case of Iowa strikes me as particularly provocative and encouraging. I base my reaction on the following facts: The setting aside of land for park and recreation purposes is relatively easy in states with spectacular (and relatively unproductive) scenery. The Grand Canyon, the Yosemite, the Cascades, Yellowstone and Teton National Parks—to name only the most spectacular—are scenic "naturals." It has also proved easy to set aside scenic areas in sparsely settled states such as Oregon, where the competition from real-estate developers is relatively mild. But it may be generalized that in Iowa nine out of every ten acres have long been under intensive cultivation and are classed as among the richest soils in the entire United States. Yet Iowa, with unspectacular scenic resources, has set aside parks and recreation areas throughout the entire state because Iowans want them. The attendance figures are impressive. In 1937 just under 2,300,000 persons visited Iowa's parks, which, it should be noted in fairness, were at the time relatively few. By 1967 the number of visitors reached 9,850,000. Overnight camping in the state's recreation areas numbered only a little under 7,000 in 1957 and had increased to 435,000 by 1967.

Because Iowa is still principally an agricultural state it is not bothered with problems which are difficult to handle in densely urbanized areas such as the eastern megalopolis strip which extends from Virginia to Maine. The main difference between these two regions is the lack of political support in the East for wise land-use planning.

While I have referred to this elsewhere in this book I mention it again here because I suspect that part of the success of Iowa's campaign for conservation is due to the fact that the state is relatively free from the pressures of real-estate developers to defeat any plans for guided land use other than their own. The premises on which Iowa based its conservation policy have no parallels among the more crowded states of the nation. This is why it is important for other states to know just what Iowa has undertaken by way of planning and implementation, and why it is equally important to watch how Iowa fares in the next two or three decades.

14

NEW HAMPSHIRE SAVES BEAUTY

ALTHOUGH New Hampshire was one of the original thirteen colonies, it is behind its sisters in density of population and ahead of them in the extensiveness of its forests. Four out of five acres in the state are tree covered—mostly second growth, although some virgin timber remains. There would be more had not the hurricane of 1938 cut a wide swath through the White Mountain National Forest and north and south of it. Second growth predominates throughout the state not only because the lumbermen had preceded the hurricane, but also because about a half of New Hampshire was farmed a century ago and when farmers went West to take up new land under the Homestead Act of 1862, New Hampshire forests reclaimed abandoned farms.

The drive from the Massachusetts border to northern New Hampshire, which I took in the autumn of 1968, was through a secluded scenic wilderness. We passed few settlements, large or small, and only an occasional farmhouse—usually unoccupied. The road was hedged in by dense second growth. Accustomed to the open-space country of the West, I remarked to my New Hampshire host, who was a trained forester, that I was surprised to see so much unused land. He replied tartly: "What do you mean 'unused'?" and explained that what I thought was unused was a crop of trees that would not mature for years but could ultimately prove profitable.

It was a pleasant wilderness, and as we moved north into higher altitudes, brilliant autumn coloring added to its charm. But it seemed as deserted as did many reaches in the "great open spaces" of the intermountain and coastal West—which suggested that large areas in this, the heart of New England, are still in a state of nature and easily accessible to millions of urban and suburban families. Lumbermen might hope to cut the second growth in the twenty-first century, but much of the land could ideally—and probably profitably—be used for recreation. Small wonder that countless Americans who live within fifty miles of the borders of New Hampshire look on that state as an ideal place for a vacation, whether in winter or summer, or for weekends. As early as 1905, when lumbering was at its height, an official report noted that visitors spent about half as much money in New Hampshire as did the entire lumber industry. Today vacationists are the state's main source of income.

In New Hampshire I was glad to renew early associations with a privately sponsored and directed organization which had taken as its title: "The Society for the Protection of New Hampshire Forests." This group has done more for a longer time to help attain conservation goals than has any other similar organization—a statement that surely merits amplification. (And let me here express my thanks to the historian of the Society, Professor Paul Bruns of the University of New Hampshire and author of *A New Hampshire Everlasting and*

Unfallen, for allowing me to read a copy of a draft of a history of the society which he was completing when I met him in New Hampshire in the autumn of 1968.)

Even the title of the society is unique in that it uses the word "protection" where other organizations would have used "preservation." I have enough New England blood in me (Connecticut Yankee) to sense that the word was picked when the society was formed in 1901 because clear-headed New Hampshire Yankees saw that "protection" was more specific and accurate than "preservation." New Hampshire's forests needed protection in 1901—protection from further destruction by lumbermen—and would long continue to need it. Preservation in those early days took for granted ultimate consumption, whereas protection as used by the New Hampshire society and many modern conservationists is based on nonconsumption. Forests are to be seen but not cut. Whether or not any of the founders expressed it in these words, the history of the society shows that it was operated on the premise that New Hampshire's protection of its forests was for the enjoyment of future as well as present users. The society's members looked on live trees as having greater potential value than the lumber that might be cut from them. As New Hampshire's forests in the early twentieth century were privately owned, the lands could be bought and sold and stripped of their trees and built upon as the owners wished. Only governments could halt such actions by incorporating the land into state or national forests. Hardly anyone in the early 1900s, either in the East or the West, had formulated the theory that trees and lakes and scenery should be protected because they formed a pleasant backdrop. Utility and prices—not appearance—were then the measures of value on a nation-wide scale. It is pertinent that even the establishment of Yellowstone and Yosemite National Parks in the last third of the nineteenth century had been urged not on the grounds of their natural beauty but rather because of their uniqueness.

Of even greater interest than the society's policies is its long record of achievement. How did it happen that a group of private citizens was able throughout seven decades to help New Hampshire and the Federal and state governments so effectively in so many good conservation causes?

An important factor in the society's success is that from the start its officers and advisers included several former state governors, such as Frank W. Rollins, who became the Society's first president; Robert P. Bass, John G. Wynant, and Roland B. Spaulding, and that the Society's directors maintained close contacts with political leaders. The mere fact that the Society favored a project or urged a policy insured prompt attention and carried weight.

The society also had close friends and advisers among professional foresters. Outstanding among these were Philip W. Ayres, who was given the position and title of "Forester" of the society in 1901 and held that office until 1935, and Edgar C. Hirst, who in 1909 had been appointed New Hampshire's first "state forester" and who, in 1950, became president of the society after having been for twenty-five years a member of its executive committee.

Ayres was born in Iowa in 1861 and had studied forestry at Cornell. He fell in love with New Hampshire and gave his long life to saving as much of its scenic heritage as possible, bringing to the Society the background of a professional forester with a flair for publicity. I had many talks with him during the 1920s, when he was struggling to save as much as possible of New Hampshire's forests and I was a member of the editorial staff of *The New York Times*. Apparently he was glad to find a youthful editorial writer on that paper whose enthusiasm for conservation was greater than his knowledge of the subject, but who was a good listener. As he talked—and I, unfortunately, failed to make notes which would have been useful forty years later—I realized that he combined hardheadedness with foresight, and that he was moved by a passion to protect New Hampshire's scenic beauties for the enjoyment and inspiration of coming generations. Ayres combined sensitivity with practicality. He knew what to protect and how to protect it, and worked hard to achieve his goal.

The importance of New Hampshire's role in the nation's conservation movement, in which once more the Society for the Protection of New Hampshire Forests had a hand, was enhanced by the part played by a New Hampshire-born man who moved to Boston in his early twenties and became congressman from Massachusetts and later United States senator and a member of the cabinet under Presidents Harding and Coolidge. This was John W. Weeks, whose home in Lancaster, New Hampshire, is now part of the state's park system.

Weeks, who was a successful businessman and political leader, is remembered as the author of what has been called for a half century "The Weeks Law," which was signed by President Taft in 1911. This law authorized the Federal government to purchase lands to be incorporated into National Forests. Prior to its passage National Forests could be created only out of land already owned by the national government, which meant that, as all the large areas of Federally owned lands were west of the Mississippi, there was no setting aside National Forests in the Eastern states even by the simple process of purchase. One of the first—and still one of the most

important—products of this law was the creation of the
White Mountain National Forest, of which 93 per cent is in
New Hampshire and the balance in Maine. The Weeks Law
provides that before the Federal government can buy land
in any state to create a National Forest the state's legislature
must enact enabling legislation. Agreement must also be
reached between levels of government to fix the boundaries
of the area in which purchases can be made. All purchases
are on the open market, without resort to eminent domain.

It is not surprising that although a similar measure had
had previous support from numerous Republicans (but had
failed to pass), the long-entrenched, ultraconservative Speaker
of the House of Representatives, commonly referred to as
"Uncle Joe" Cannon, regarded the project as a dangerous in-
novation. Uncle Joe is reported to have said of the Weeks
Law that "A new departure in government and legislation
once begun, there is no telling where it will stop"—a typical
conservative reaction of those days in which conservatives
were convinced that innovations were to be viewed with suspicion, carefully examined, and sternly resisted if there
seemed to be even a chance that they might "put ideas" in
the minds of reformers.

Congressman Weeks's son, Sinclair, who later, like his father, was senator from Massachusetts, and subsequently served
as Secretary of Commerce, told me in the autumn of 1968
that when the elder Weeks was first elected to Congress,
"Uncle Joe" had sent for him to tell him that he, the Speaker,
had named Weeks a member of the Committee on Agriculture. When Congressman Weeks remarked that he held views
that differed from those of "Uncle Joe," and that they might
find themselves opposed, the Speaker replied that if the congressman could win over the Committee on Agriculture to a

bill in behalf of acquiring private lands for incorporation into national forests, he (Speaker Cannon) would not oppose passage of the bill.

In a letter which Congressman Weeks wrote to Gifford Pinchot, a year after the Weeks Law was passed, the congressman reported that the Speaker said to him: "I am not putting you on the Agriculture Committee because I expect you to make my views yours. In fact I would not put you there, or give you any other position of responsibility if I thought you would, and I want to say this: that if you can frame a forestry bill which you as a businessman are willing to put forward I will do what I can to get it consideration in the House."

As one who has long watched the American political scene closely, and in particular, the swings of the Republican party between the pseudo radicalism of the elder and the two younger LaFollettes on the left and the ultraconservatism of Old Guard Republicans with "Uncle Joe" on the right, I am inclined to think that the quotation attributed to Speaker Cannon about establishing a bad precedent accurately expressed his political philosophy. Cannon obviously feared that if the precedent of buying lands for incorporation into National Forests was established it would make it easier to obtain money for other even more undesirable sociological experiments.

On re-examining the Weeks Law I am struck with its emphasis on the value of watersheds of navigable rivers rather than on the importance of acquiring National Forests in Eastern states. The chances are that it would have been hard to obtain passage of this bill if its purpose had been labeled: "to acquire forest lands as part of an overall program of conservation." Navigable rivers were regarded in the early 1900s as still worthy of protection and development, even though their value was beginning to be questioned. Vote-conscious members of Congress could acquire political merit by supporting them. But the purchase of privately owned tree-covered land to be included in new National Forests had few friends among conservative Republicans in a Congress still smarting from the way Theodore Roosevelt and Gifford Pinchot had fooled them in 1908 by setting aside millions of acres of public lands as National Forests in the last ten days before the President's power to do so was abrogated. There were few votes for saving trees in the early 1900s, and as is pointed out in Chapter II, the mere fact that Theodore Roosevelt wanted to save trees was enough to induce old-line Republicans to sacrifice them.

The Society for the Protection of New Hampshire Forests helped stimulate interest in the passage of the Weeks Law and worked hard in behalf of the establishment of the White Mountain National Forest. The success of the society's efforts may be judged from a letter addressed to Mr. Ayres, when he retired as forester of the society, by Henry S. Graves, former chief of the U. S. Forest Service and at the time dean of the Yale School of Forestry. It read: "You did more than anyone else to bring about passage of the Weeks Law. That is one of the epoch-making measures of forest history. You made the White Mountain National Forest possible. It stands as a monument to your creative efforts. I do not overlook what you have done in building up one of the most influential local agencies for the expression of public opinion in the country."

Of a later vintage than Ayres was Edgar C. Hirst who, as I pointed out, became New Hampshire's first state forester in 1909 and was president of the Society for the Protection of New Hampshire Forests from 1950 until 1966. He was in his mid-eighties when I met him in October 1968, and was still deeply interested in the cause to which he had given his long and successful career. His detailed knowledge of what the state government could do and of the help which it needed was of value to the society during the years in which he was one of its most effective officers. No wonder that an organization that had so many leaders who had been active in state administration and politics was able to play such a constructive role.

I stress this aspect of the work of the society not only because of the society's success but because if that organization had not existed, and if it had not had so many close ties with the state's political leaders, much of New Hampshire's rich scenic heritage would long since have been lost. The Society for the Protection of New Hampshire's Forests, like the Save-the-Redwoods League, has shown clearly that a determined group of influential citizens can do much to guide and help a state administration achieve valuable goals.

The other important lesson of this New Hampshire society is that conservation wars may be won but peace is not self-sustaining, and that, as in so many military wars, geography can play an influential part. For years the society had fought to protect the region around Franconia Notch, which is one of the most spectacular parts of the White Mountains, and even though severe damage had been done to parts of its natural cover by lumbermen and by forest fires in the critical era when protection was most needed, the Notch and its surroundings were finally acquired, partly by the state and partly by the society after prolonged negotiations. Conservationists felt secure in their victory.

Then one day surveyors arrived in the Franconia Notch

region with transits and stakes brought in by trucks bearing the insignia of the New Hampshire Department of Public Works and Highways. The engineers forthwith began staking out what they considered to be the best location for a major north-south interstate throughway. Their procedure followed the Department's usual practice, which seems to be based on the proposition that the engineers can do no wrong and that, therefore, their plans are not to be questioned. What they want will be done. What they wanted in this case was the Notch.

They wanted this because geography had made plain that this pass was the best within many miles through which a major north-south throughway could be built at reasonable cost. Despite the strong opposition of the state park authorities and of the Society, as well as of many other groups and individuals, the pressures in behalf of building it proved almost irresistible, even though the area would be severely scarred.

The incident is a sad reminder that conflict of interests between road builders and conservationists is often irreconcilable. Highway engineers think in terms of safety, speed, and cost. Conservationists think in terms of saving spectacular portions of the nation's scenic heritage. The engineers naturally emphasize the interrelationship between the lay of the land and safety, both of which can greatly affect cost. They usually choose the less expensive of possible alternate routes, unless the evidence is clear that the cheaper route is likely to be more accident prone. A large and steadily growing motoring public, accustomed to driving at legal speed limits of sixty or seventy miles an hour, is likely to resent and ignore warnings to reduce speeds at particular curves unless traffic

is so dense that it is virtually impossible for them to maintain—or exceed—the posted limits.

Thanks to the initiative of the New Hampshire state government and private organizations, studies were made by disinterested highway consultants for alternate routes. Public
hearings were held. In 1966 the governor appointed a special
committee to consider all aspects of the Franconia problem
and approved a plan submitted by the state's Department of
Public Works and Highways for a tunnel through the heart
of the Notch—a project still under consideration when this
chapter was written. As an outsider with no engineering training I find it hard to see why through traffic could not by-pass
the Notch by a longer route at a substantial distance from it.
Even if such a detour added fifteen or twenty miles to a
through trip, it would lengthen by only fifteen to twenty minutes the traveling time of a car adhering to the usual speed
limits. The Good Lord spent centuries sculpting the Notch,
yet modern tourists and truckers presumably cannot be asked
to spare twenty minutes extra travel time to by-pass—and
save—it.

Another accomplishment of New Hampshire in the overall
field of conservation was to adapt Massachusetts' example of
authorizing "Community Conservation Commissions." These
have as their purpose the protection of natural resources at
the local levels. It is to New Hampshire's credit that the people were quick to see the advantages of having local committees take an active part in planning for protection, as well as
development, of local communities. Under legislation enacted
by the New Hampshire general court (which is the equivalent
of what in most other states is called the state legislature),
local conservation commissions are empowered to make studies of local needs and possibilities of the preservation or use

of natural resources, and may recommend to the local selectmen positive measures. The existence of these local commissions has facilitated intelligent study and has helped win local
support for, and participation in, sound community decisions
about the preservation of local resources. The legislation,
which is permissive, enables local units to survey open space
areas for possible conservation use; to coordinate activities of
nongovernmental bodies having conservation goals in mind;
to receive gifts of money or property to be managed by the
commission; and to request technical assistance from the New
Hampshire Department of Resources and Economic Development in acquiring land and in planning use. In other
words, these conservation commissions are literally grassroots
groups empowered to consider problems of community amen-
ities and appearances—something new in the American political structure and a far step from the purely administrative
duties of officials in New England towns in the days before
the Revolution. Legislation for formation of these conservation commissions was supported by the Society for the Protection of New Hampshire Forests, and endorsed by the Audubon Society of New Hampshire, the New Hampshire Natural
Resources Council, and various other groups. The widespread support in the state for the designation of these local
advisory groups has done much to center interest on local
problems of conservation. As yet the commissions in New
Hampshire have moved slowly, and in numerous instances,
effectively.

The problem of projected real-estate developments is, of
course, ever present, and usually full of potential threats to
the survival of open space. Yet in at least one instance—usually referred to as the Asquam Lake Ski and Beach Club proposal—the combined action of residents and officials of a num-

ber of New Hampshire towns in the neighborhood of Squam Lake managed to discourage the completion of a development project which not only would have changed the character of that lake—one of the most beautiful in the state—but also would almost surely have resulted in the pollution of the lake's waters, which till then had been notoriously clean. In brief, the developers, who took the name of "Asquam Lake Ski and Beach Club," acquired 230 acres, some of which abutted on the lake, which they planned to subdivide into 600 lots, with docking facilities, clubhouse, and swimming pool. The developers, who were nonresidents and presumably not well-informed about New Hampshire laws, laid out a road and dumped a lot of fill into the lake.

When the selectmen (who are the counterparts of town and county officials in most other states) became concerned about this, a meeting was organized in Concord at which were present representatives from the State Water Resources Board, the State Water Pollution Control Commission, the Fish and Game Department, the State Planning Office, the U. S. Soil Conservation Service, representatives from the state legislature and selectmen from Center Harbor, the town in which the project was located.

At the meeting, which lasted four hours, attention centered primarily on the danger of pollution of the lake's waters. The representative of the U. S. Soil Conservation Service testified that over half the soils in the proposed development had hard pan at about eighteen inches below the surface, which meant that water or drainage penetrating to this depth could move only laterally, with the result that the sewage would end up in the lake, thus depriving the lake of one of its greatest assets—the purity of its water.

A few days later the local press reported that five towns

adjoining Squam Lake were seeking a permanent injunction to stop further development of this proposed project until adequate provision could be made for suitable sewage disposal. The injunction also was to put an end to filling any portion of the lake and stressed the fact that the developers had dumped many cubic yards of fill in the bed of the lake in violation of existing state laws.

The Water Resources Board then took direct action. The site was surveyed and land ownership clearly defined, and all fill in the lake was ordered removed. Thanks to the intercession of many citizens the governor and council agreed with the Water Resources Board's recommendation that the petition of the realtors to build in the area be denied. Shortly thereafter the project was abandoned.

Superficially this proposed development resembled thousands of real-estate operations planned or completed elsewhere in the nation. But at issue at Squam Lake was the probable long-range effects of this project, not only by polluting the waters of the lake but by filling part of it, thus altering its appearance and incidentally reducing the area of a long-established migratory bird sanctuary. The fact that local officials welcomed direct assistance and advice of Federal as well as state and local bodies strengthened the hands of conservationists within the state and gave new evidence of the value of active concern on the part of local interests to halt unplanned and uncoordinated suburbanization in a purely rural area.

In discussing this case with Mr. Randall P. Raymond, assistant planning director in the New Hampshire Department of Resources and Economic Development, he pointed out that it played a catalytic role in the adoption of a major anti-pollution bill by the New Hampshire general court in 1967.

The proposed legislation received active support from various state agencies and from the Federal government. Citizens' groups joined in urging strong control of land development around the state's lakes. Desire to protect the appearance of the lakes was widely expressed, obviously in the conviction that they are among the state's major scenic assets.

The amount of space which I have devoted to the activities of organizations and individuals in behalf of conservation in New Hampshire is not in any way intended as a reflection on state officials and administrators. Not only have political leaders, including a number of able governors, done all in their power to implement sound conservation practices in New Hampshire during the last seventy years, but the state government has placed in key positions such as state forester, and the Office of Planning and Research, men and women of outstanding ability. This last-named office has been held since 1960 by Miss Mary Louise Hancock, who has brought to her work imagination and shrewd judgment of policies and possibilities. Planning, as defined in the legislation establishing the department of which the Office of Planning and Research is a part, covers a large field, including the encouragement of the development of industry, recreation, and agriculture as well as the promotion of public health, safety, convenience, and general welfare. The office participates in interstate, regional, and national planning efforts—which suggests that for a relatively understaffed department of a state government it has its hands full. In my brief contact with Miss Hancock and her assistants I was struck not only with their ability and knowledge, but also with the apparently close relations that exist between this office and such organizations as the Audubon Society, the Society for the Protection of New Hampshire Forests, the New Hampshire Natural Resources Council, the New Hampshire Natural Preserves Forum, and the New England Wild Flower Preservation Society. They share the common goal of saving New Hampshire's beauty. Certainly if other states' governments and nongovernmental groups worked together so harmoniously, the cause of conservation throughout the nation would be greatly advanced.

15

MAKE STRAIGHT A HIGHWAY

Although the routing of freeways is not governed by concepts of conservation, there have been times when a proposed location of a freeway has aroused strong and justifiable protests from conservationists.

Consider the case of Colby College in Maine.

Colby is a relatively small New England college in Waterville, founded in 1813. It ranks high among educational institutions. Probably its best-known graduate was Elijah Lovejoy, who edited a small newspaper in Alton, Illinois, and was killed by a mob in 1837 because he refused to keep silent in the face of threats of slavery racketeers who could only silence him by killing him. But Colby has graduated many other men of distinction in many lines during the last century and a half.

Colby's original campus became hemmed in by factories and warehouses because it was small and near the railway, which did not reach Waterville until after the college had been well established. After World War II, Colby graduates raised enough money to move the college to Mayflower Hill near the outskirts of the town. There a beautiful new campus was laid out and dormitories and other needed structures were built. The college authorities were widely praised for their good taste in the design of the campus and the buildings. They had reason to believe that, at least insofar as location was concerned, their troubles were at an end.

But in the month of August 1956 college officials were first puzzled and then worried by the presence of surveyors on the campus sent in by the State of Maine Highway Commission, then engaged in planning the route of the Augusta-Benton superhighway, which was to be one of the main links in the Atlantic Coast north-and-south superhighway chain.

Incredible as it now seems, the route which the highway engineers chose cut straight through the heart of Colby's campus and the grounds of the nearby Thayer Hospital. In a press release a spokesman for the State Highway Commission explained that this line was the best of several routes considered by the highway engineers.

Officials and alumni of Colby College, backed by local leaders and by spokesmen for other New England colleges, protested the proposed route of the highway. Public meetings were held and the State Highway Commission agreed to study alternative routes, one of which lay to the west of the campus. The engineers insisted that the route bisecting the campus was the best. Finally, a representative of the Bureau of Public Roads in Washington, which was paying nine tenths of the cost of the throughway, announced at a meeting that the Bureau had decided definitely to go straight through the campus and would not even consider any alternative route.

The meeting broke up in an uproar and there followed months of talks between spokesmen for Colby and officials in

Washington and Augusta. In April 1957 the Federal Bureau of Public Roads formally rejected the so-called compromise route, which followed the western border of the campus and which had relatively little opposition from the college and local people. Protests and discussion continued throughout the summer, and finally resulted in the Federal bureau abandoning its stubborn stand. I was told by a friend who had been in the campaign that the determining factor was a statement pointing out that the compromise along the western boundary of the campus would lengthen by only a little more than one minute the travel time of a car obeying the speed limit through the Waterville area.

In fairness to highway engineers, whether in Washington, or the state of Maine, or California, or elsewhere, two points should be stressed: (1) Engineers are governed by statutes and regulations and by strictly defined appropriations. Their duty is to hold down costs to predetermined figures and to abide by rigid engineering standards as to grades, curves, roadside slopes, and the width of rights of way. Even if highway engineers might like to by-pass some particular area for aesthetic or other reasons, they lack the authority to do so. (2) Long experience has taught highway engineers that each decision to widen or realign an existing road or to construct a new highway meets with virtually unanimous opposition on the part of property owners along or near the desired right of way. As a result, the engineers become hardened to criticism and opposition and find it easier to stand pat than to consider changes, knowing that any changes will, in turn, meet fresh opposition from new sources. As trained technicians the engineers' concern is with practical problems and with costs rather than with public relations. Such blame as may be apportioned should therefore go to those who planned the original routing rather than to the men in charge of the actual survey and construction, and these planners are almost always limited by factors other than aesthetics.

The Colby case is dramatic but not unique. The mere fact that it ended in an acceptable compromise is more important than the initial effrontery or stupidity of the engineers. It is of special concern to conservationists for two reasons: (1) It points up the fact that highways can endanger, and even ruin, theoretically impregnable oases of preservation; and (2) it shows that an aroused citizenry fighting in a good cause can win.

A somewhat similar instance occurred in New Mexico a few years after the Colby College case. This involved not only the government of the state of New Mexico but also two bureaus of the Federal government and centered on a project of the New Mexico State Highway Division to widen and realign one of the two main roads between Santa Fe and the famous Indian village of Taos. An old two-lane wagon road on the western slope of the Sangre de Cristo mountain range which, in turn, forms the eastern boundary of the valley of the Rio Grande in this part of New Mexico, passed near a small village known as Las Trampas. This has a particularly fine Spanish adobe church built in 1751. The villagers early became affiliated with the sect known as the "Penitentes," which was made up of persons obsessed with a strong sense of sin, who periodically subjected themselves to severe discipline by way of penance. Even among the Spanish stock in Santa Fe, the people who live on the slope of the Sangre de Cristo range were regarded with tolerance and respect by their fellow Spanish-Americans. All that the residents of Las Trampas wanted was to live their own lives in their own way, without regard to their Anglo-American neighbors.

But the New Mexico Highway Division had plans of its own for these villagers. It decided to realign the old dirt road and make it into a three-lane paved highway with a sixty foot right of way. As the realigned road approached Las Trampas it would obliterate most of the plaza and the churchyard and pass to within three feet of the wall of the church. Apparently the Spanish-American engineers of the Highway Division who were staking out the route of the realigned highway assured the local residents that the change in width and location of the new road would bring tourists to the area and that it presaged a period of prosperity in the village. None of the villagers seemed interested in the fate of the church.

As often happens in such cases, outsiders heard about what the planned changes would do to the fine old Spanish church of Las Trampas. They suggested the simple solution of retaining the location of the old road as it approached the village of Las Trampas, leaving the plaza, churchyard, and mission as they had always been.

One of the members and organizers of the group sponsoring the saving of Las Trampas was the famous architect, planner, and author, Nathaniel A. Owings, who later had a major part in the rehabilitation of Pennslyavnia Avenue in Washington, D.C. He and some friends organized the Las Trampas Foundation to save the village and church. To a layman their suggested procedure seemed as simple as it was sensible. But, as Owings explained to me, four government units would have to agree even to such a simple procedure. The county, the state of New Mexico, the U.S. Department of Transportation, and the U.S. Department of the Interior would all have to play a definite role. The county neither opposed nor endorsed the suggested change. The New Mexico highway engineers did what all other highway engineers would do under such circumstances—resisted having their alignments questioned or changed. Usually when a highway division takes such a stand it has its way and no bureaucracy— least of all a division of highways—likes to admit the possibility of error. In this case the only way in which the engineers could be enjoined would be to have Las Trampas church and environs designated as a national historic site.

If this could be done the provision of an existing Federal law could be invoked which was designed to prevent the engineers from invading and injuring such a National Historic Site in the aligning or rebuilding of a highway.

A number of the key people in the Las Trampas Foundation knew that the National Park Service in Washington had a commission which passed on the qualification of any particular area to be officially designated as a National Historic Site. The foundation, therefore, got in touch with the National Park Service (providentially, the active director in charge of the Foundation was a former National Park Service officer). The Historic Sites Commission was impressed with the importance of saving Las Trampas, and after a thorough study, recommended that it be given the status of a National Historic Site. The Department of Transportation, which was helping to implement the State of New Mexico's plan for the realignment of the road, requested reconsideration of the matter.

Accordingly, the Secretary of the Interior and the Secretary of Transportation agreed that a conference should be held in New Mexico at which representatives from the various interested bureaus and other groups should discuss the proposal.

At the meeting, which was held in Santa Fe, the Secretary of Transportation was represented by his deputy, Mr. Fred S. Farr, who for years had been a member of the California

State Senate, and actively interested in many conservation causes. By chance he was an old friend and associate of Mr. Owings, who had been a prime mover in the attempt to save Las Trampas. The Park Service was represented, as was the National Historic Sites Board. So also, several representatives from the government of the state of New Mexico attended, as did officials of the Las Trampas Foundation. The archbishop of Santa Fe expressed his approval of the plan to save Las Trampas.

Out of this meeting came an agreement to accept the suggestion that on the stretch of the new road approaching the church the alignment of the original old road should be followed, thus saving the plaza and churchyard. Furthermore, the road was to retain its old two-lane width as it passed the church. A new timber bridge was to be built across the Las Trampas creek with special facilities to enable the villagers to water their stock as they had done for generations, instead of following the engineers' plan to place the stream in a culvert and bury the culvert with a big fill. The Las Trampas Foundation financed the recoating of the church in adobe of the original color, and restored the church's two wooden towers which had been removed a century or more ago. The Foundation also repaired the old mission bells which had remained unused for many decades.

The church was saved and the village preserved in its original form as a fine specimen of Spanish-American culture. As in so many instances, the project took much time and effort and involved substantial financial contributions from private sources. It could probably not have succeeded except for the fact that the preservationists were men who were highly regarded in Washington.

In the Colby case it was a Federal bureau that was the potential destroyer, as it was also in the Las Trampas case. Likewise, in California there have been occasions when state highway engineers have sought to locate parts of a freeway inside the boundaries of a state park, ignoring the fact that state parks are set aside expressly to save their scenic resources undamaged.

To laymen the fact that a state division of highways has a *right* to run a freeway through a park does not mean that the division is *obliged* to do so. The provision is permissive, not mandatory. Yet in California's case the Division of Highways is politically powerful and to date has resisted efforts to deprive it of this right, not so much because it expects to exercise it freely as because cases arise in which to be able to violate the territorial integrity of a park might simplify some of the engineers' problems. Furthermore, it should not be overlooked that no bureaucracy likes to surrender any of its prerogatives if it can avoid so doing.

Unfortunately, there have been instances in California when the engineers caused irreparable damage to state parks before they could be stopped—as witness the attempt to force a freeway through Humboldt State Redwood Park near the Avenue of the Giants. At least two other potentially destructive intrusions have not yet been abandoned, and if the engineers proceed, they will ruin valuable stands of fine old redwoods.

Vigorous protests from conservationists and others have been effective against this sort of bureaucratic vandalism. In a recent threat to Prairie Creek State Redwood Park in California the Division of Highways was willing to consider alternative public routes and held public hearings—perhaps because the engineers knew that local opinion supported them in their opposition to the so-called ridge route, which the conservationists wanted. This route by-passes the park, following close to the park's eastern boundary. A report of the hearings indicates that the Division of Highways presented three alternate routes: the first bisecting the park; the second running along the park's splendid Gold Bluff Beach; the third is mentioned above, which lies just east of the park. The engineers favored cutting through the park with a four-lane highway and a broad right of way. This would have made a wide swath through splendid stands of redwoods which had been included in the park in the belief and expectation that they would there be forever safe from destruction. The engineers' second choice was for running the highway along Gold Bluff Beach, one of the finest of the relatively few beaches in California owned by the state. Their third alternative was the ridge route, just outside the eastern border of the park. The engineers knew that this route was particularly objectionable from the point of view of the lumber interests who were known to have great influence in the community, and as the engineers also opposed it they are believed to have hoped that widespread local opposition to the ridge route would make it easier for them to have their way.

At the meeting the beach route turned out to be the favorite of the majority of the local people. Their second choice was for bisecting the park. Hardly any local support appeared for the ridge route. The fact that the ridge route would have cost substantially more than the beach route strengthened local opposition to it, even though the cost would have been borne by the Federal and state governments, so that the ridge route would not have added to the financial burden of the community. The ridge route would, however, involve acquisition of a right of way by the state. This brought forth the usual argument when a road is projected—

that as the land within the right of way would be taken off the county tax rolls, the county's income would be reduced accordingly. When it was pointed out that the loss to the county would amount to only about a hundred dollars a year, there was no diminution in the local opposition. Incidentally, it is interesting to note that if the right of way for the ridge route averaged an eighth of a mile in width, the total distance of this route meant that the land which would be taken off the county tax roll would amount to only a fraction of 1 per cent of the total taxable area in the county.

It was, of course, to be expected that the lumbermen would oppose the ridge route because it is several miles longer than either park route and reaches a maximum elevation several hundred feet higher than the road bisecting the park. Obviously this implies increased cost of trucking. But it would require more convincing evidence than has yet been produced to be able to equate the increased cost to a particular trucker with the increased benefits to tens of thousands of tourists if all of the trucking were to be kept out of the park.

The battle of highways versus parks is not yet over, and the odds continue to favor the highway engineers, not because their cause is sound but because they have more political influence. Highway engineers throughout the nation can count on the support of the many large industries which supply road builders with equipment and raw materials. These groups make a point of winning the friendship of local politicians, who, in turn, have influence with politicians at the state level and even higher. On the side of the parks are not only the National Park Service and most of the higher-ups among state park officials, but also conservationists who feel strongly that national and state parks should be scenic sanctuaries, and that to run heavily traveled freeways through them is against the national interests. This in no sense discourages highway engineers from considering projects for routing a new major freeway through a national or state park if the location has engineering advantages. But the fact remains that there is a basic incompatibility between the setting aside of particular areas for permanent preservation as national or state parks, and then permitting the intrusion into these areas of such completely nonpark functions as the carrying of a large volume of through traffic. The problem is sure to arise frequently in the future. When this happens it will be well if conservationists band together in memory of Hetch Hetchy, which stands out as a precedent for all would-be invaders of parks for nonpark purposes.

Defenders of parks are so sure that their cause is sound that they often fail to realize that the protection of parks calls for eternal vigilance. This is as true of urban parks as of state and national parks. One of the sharpest memories that I have of the late great Adolph S. Ochs, who made *The New York Times* into the nation's leading newspaper, was his relentless opposition to demands of would-be invaders of Central Park in New York for nonpark purposes—demands for memorial buildings, or places of entertainment, or ball grounds, or other similar intrusions. I am sure that if he had had *The New York Times* when the Metropolitan Museum of Art was being planned he would have opposed placing it inside the park boundaries, where it takes up acres of park space. This would not have been because he disapproved of the Museum as an institution, but because he did not think that it should occupy even a limited area of Central Park, and he knew that once an exception for use of Central Park was made for nonpark purposes it would be increasingly difficult to keep out other intrusions.

Excluding throughways from parks is, of course, an important form of conservation. But it is, in a sense, negative. More positive is the growing interest in beautification, and in the development of roads outside of parks for enjoyment and recreation rather than primarily for commercial transportation. It is interesting in this connection to reread the report made forty years ago by Frederick Law Olmsted, Jr., about California's park and recreation problems to which I refer in Chapter XII. In this he insisted that certain roads should be laid out to meet the demands of the motoring public for the enjoyment of scenery, and that these roads should be engineered with a view to saving the scenery rather than to despoiling it in the name of economy. To the modern lay mind this concept seems so sound that it is hard to realize that neither then nor now has it had much impact on the thinking of highway engineers and planners. Yet the concept of scenic highways—call them scenic roads, scenic drives, or parkways if you will—is more important now than ever, and for the first time since Olmsted first wrote about it, is beginning to receive favorable attention.

Looked at from the point of view of overall problems of conservation, one of the most striking things in Olmsted's analysis is that from beginning to end of a report which ran into almost a hundred pages he linked recreation with the enjoyment of scenery and rarely mentioned one without spelling out the other. In fact, he did this so often that it is clear that he considered the interrelationship of prime importance. Long before automobiles had come into the kind of mass use to which we are accustomed, he forecast that what he called "riding for no other purpose but the enjoyment of the pleasant out-of-doors" would become a major interest for millions of Americans. This, I repeat, was in 1928. He foresaw that the demands for the enjoyment of the out-of-doors would increase greatly and rapidly. In retrospect one of the most interesting points that he developed in his analysis of this aspect of recreation was his insistence that "the vast amount of enjoyment of the scenic resources of California which people get simply from riding in automobiles on public roads is essentially independent in most cases of the ownership of adjoining land. It has been well said: 'the land belongs to the owner; the landscape to him who for the moment enjoys it.' " He elaborated this point by stressing the fact that landscapes can be and are enjoyed by the public without trespass, and also without the slightest conflict between such public enjoyment and the private economic uses of the land. In other words, he recognized that the public enjoyment of scenery did not imply the need for public acquisition of that scenery.

His awareness of the value of driving for pleasure and recreation also led him to stress the need for roadside beautification long before this idea had a White House blessing and congressional approval. Not only did he urge that when highways were to be built in scenic areas they should be built with due regard to scenery, but he went so far as to urge the control of the foreground—I quote: "the foreground of the more notable and valuable landscapes enjoyable from the road—especially in those places where there is great danger of great scenic losses through lack of control." He also stressed the scenic advantages of widening highway rights of way and of establishing what he called "park" strips publicly owned and maintained along the highway. This led him to discuss concepts of what we now call scenic easements and open space, under which landowners agree to leave the landscape along a public road unchanged, without foregoing the agricultural uses of the land.

While much progress has been made in the development of state parks since he first advanced these novel concepts, relatively little has been done by the highway builders of the nation to implement his sound concept of the close relationship between recreation and scenery, and between driving for pleasure and the beautification of the highway environment.

I re-emphasize this point not in a spirit of criticism of highway engineers, but rather because I feel that Olmsted clearly pointed up one of the hitherto neglected facets of the overall problems of conservation. It is, of course, true that there are large areas in the United States where due either to suburbanization or to the relative flatness or drabness of the landscape, the corridors along the two sides of a highway hold little to challenge the attention of vacationists. But it is also true that even outside of parks there are many sections of the countryside through which fine roads have been built which add materially to the enjoyment of persons driving over them for recreation purposes. And it must not be overlooked that driving for pleasure still heads the list of the most popular means of recreation throughout nearly all of the United States.

WANTED: MORE GIANTS

THE Save-the-Redwoods League has been described as "one of the most phenomenally successful conservation organizations in history." Certainly its record is impressive. In the half century of its life it has planned, negotiated, and financed the purchase of thousands of acres of fine old coast redwoods, and has deeded these to the state of California for preservation as state parks. The present value of the redwood groves that the League acquired for the state has been estimated at $250,000,000. As California had no state park system when the League began to buy trees, it faced the problem of what could be done to protect the lands which it turned over to the state. The obvious long-term solution was for the state to set up a bureau or a commission to administer park lands and to develop an overall state park and recreation policy. This the League fostered, and although it cannot claim sole credit for what has become California's state park system, it helped interest influential persons in the need for establishing an adequate administrative body and an efficient park and recrea-

185

tion service. The Save-the-Redwoods League is one of the few nongovernmental organizations which played a major part in the setting up of a new government bureau to help in the development of a new function of government.

Despite the League's ultimate preeminence in the saving of redwoods, it was neither the first nor the only worker in this field. As early as 1901—sixteen years before the League had even been thought of—a group in Santa Cruz calling itself the Sempervirens Club helped to establish the first redwood state park in California—Big Basin. This was, of course, before the state had any park system. In 1908, thanks to the generosity of Congressman William Kent of Marin County, the fine grove of coast redwoods just north of San Francisco, now known as "The Muir Woods" was given to the Federal government, and was set aside by President Theodore Roosevelt as a national monument—the first and only time that the bureau which was to become the National Park Service was given jurisdiction over a fine stand of coast redwoods. A few years later some ladies of Eureka in the northern part of California arranged for preserving some fine groves nearby. These efforts, both north and south, were, however, spasmodic and uncoordinated.

The impetus for the formation of the Save-the-Redwoods League is generally credited to three men who camped together in the redwoods in Humboldt county in the first week of August 1917, reputedly at the suggestion of Stephen T. Mather, then director of the National Park Service. These men—Madison Grant, president of the New York Zoological Society; Henry Fairfield Osborn, head of the Museum of Natural History in New York City; and John C. Merriam, of the University of California, later head of the Carnegie Institution, became convinced that as many as possible of the

groves of large old coast redwoods must be saved as parks and
discussed how this could best be done. Records of their talks
are few, which is a pity, as they were men of vision. The
League's success goes back to their foresight, intelligence,
perseverance, and sense of responsibility.

Madison Grant was deeply sensitive to natural beauty, a
great outdoors man with strong prejudices, some good, some
bad. When I met him in 1928 he was old, crotchety, and
twisted with arthritis, but still fighting valiantly to save redwoods. Because of his friendship for Theodore Roosevelt and
for my father—the three were fellow members of the Boone
and Crockett Club, of which Grant was president when he
died—he overlooked the fact that he and I differed on most
things other than the saving of redwoods.

In contrast to Grant, Dr. Osborn was urbane and tolerant,
a coordinator rather than an innovator, accustomed to
achievement. His many influential friends in the East, and
the respect in which he was held, were of help to the League.
In my talks with him I found him imaginative and constructive.

I never met Dr. Merriam, but those who knew him told me
that he worked creatively and effectively with Grant and Osborn and did much to help organize and launch the League.
He was one of its early presidents. Among other incorporators
were Franklin K. Lane, Secretary of the Interior under President Wilson; William E. Colby, secretary and later president
of the Sierra Club and the first chairman of the California
State Park Commission; Henry S. Graves, chief of the U. S.
Forest Service; Stephen T. Mather, director of the National
Park Service; Benjamin Ide Wheeler, president of the University of California; Robert G. Sproul, who later held that
same office; Ray Lyman Wilbur, president of Leland Stan-

ford, Jr., University and later Secretary of the Interior under President Hoover; and William H. Crocker, San Francisco financier and civic leader. Little wonder that an organization formed by such men accomplished as much as did the Save-the-Redwoods League. Its directors had access to fruitful sources of funds, and friends among politicians, editors, and publicists. The mere fact that such men backed the saving of redwoods was in itself news. The League got off to a good start.

In looking over the records of the League I was struck with the fact that at one of the first meetings of its directors the League's aims were set forth as being (I quote from the minutes): "(a) To secure the finest and most available tracts of redwoods as a national park. (b) To secure a strip three hundred yards wide or other suitable width along each side of the highway as a state park. (c) To obtain by private gifts such other fine tracts of land which may be recommended by a committee appointed to make a study of the situation." Two and a half weeks later the directors appointed a committee with duties to "formulate and present a plan for securing the best and most valuable tract of redwood timber for reservation as a national park. This committee also to act for the redwoods League in putting the proposed plan of action into effect after approval by the executive committee." It is pertinent to note that this committee a half century ago found that no national park could be set up without an act of Congress which, in turn, had to be supplemented by an appropriation to buy the land, and that Congress showed little interest in implementing either suggestion. In theory the argument was, then as now, that large stands of the finest old coast redwoods belonged in a national park. These trees were among the wonders of the world. As it would cost much to buy them, and as their preservation concerned the nation as a whole, and not California alone, it was logical that the Federal government should finance such a park, and obviously it would be easier for Congress to vote the funds than it would be for California to do so. Furthermore, the state of California as yet had no park system. The raising of large sums to buy redwoods would present difficult administrative and financial problems for the state government.

It is easy to say now that it would have been ideal if a redwood national park had been established a half century ago, as the Redwoods League initially suggested. But this was not done. This failure is all the more regrettable in that the revival in the 1960s of nation-wide interest in the establishment of a redwoods national park came at a time when prospects of funds for such a project were dim. With the nation caught in a costly war in Asia and torn by civil strife at home almost as grave as when Abraham Lincoln became president, it was not likely that Congress would appropriate $175,000,000—or even half that sum—to buy old trees. The situation was confused by honest differences of opinion among partisans of different areas who believed that these should be included in a national park. This lack of harmony played into the hands of the lumber industry, which, opposed alike to the creation of a national park and of more state parks, was glad to see the Federal and state governments at odds and the conservationists disunited. While officials sparred, and a Sierra Club publicity agent belittled the Save-the-Redwoods League, it is to the League's credit that its guiding principle remained unchanged: to seek to save as many of the finest old redwoods as practicable, rather than to fight stubbornly for inclusion of a particular area.

This attitude of the League's directors stems from the

League's early days. The founders were men of action. Their concern was to save the best groves of redwoods which could be got, and they were not distracted from their goal by arguments about custodial jurisdiction. When they saw that the Federal government was not interested in a national park, and that the state government lacked the machinery as well as the money to buy redwood groves for the state, they championed the obvious alternative—that groves of suitable character be bought through private gifts. This meant that the League must learn where the best stands of old trees were, who owned them, and how much—or rather how little—they would cost. The League must then raise money to buy them.

It was at this juncture that the directors of the League found for the position of executive secretary a sound judge of good redwoods, who became a shrewd negotiator for their purchase, and was an effective money raiser. This man was Newton B. Drury, who joined the League Staff in 1919, shortly after its inception as an active organization, and was its mainspring until 1940, when he was appointed director of the National Park Service in Washington under the irrascible but able Secretary of the Interior, Harold L. Ickes. Drury held this post for eleven years and then for nine years was director of California's Division of Beaches and Parks in Sacramento. That he filled these two important government offices is a measure of his capabilities, and added to his knowledge and experience. It was the League's further good fortune that when he retired as head of the California Division of Beaches and Parks in 1959 he resumed his old office as executive secretary of the Save-the-Redwoods League. While he was in Washington and Sacramento his brother, Aubrey, served as executive secretary of the League, and effectively helped acquire important stands of redwoods. It was largely under Aubrey's leadership that the establishment of memorial groves was successfully developed. My guess is that the League and California's Division of Beaches and Parks both profited from the coincidence that two brothers ran these two organizations.

Newton Drury's work called for a combination of shrewdness, patience, energy, perseverance, and tact. He had to hike over miles of mountains and through groves full of down timber and did this in a part of California which a half century ago was still close to the old frontier. His dealings were with lumbermen absorbed in the mechanics of felling trees—men who were puzzled, worried, and annoyed by the idea that sound groves of fine old trees should be saved for posterity. A tree was to be cut, and the lumber from it to be milled. Conservation as we think of it was alien to their way of life. Furthermore, they were wary of wanderers from the outside world, and were ill at ease with college-bred city folk. In this atmosphere Drury had to find the trees he wanted, placate the owners, get the O.K. of the League's directors and help raise money to buy the approved groves. He had then to undertake extensive negotiations leading to the state's agreement to match dollar for dollar the gifts which the League obtained.

Of importance in assessing the role of the League is the fact that it antedated by nine years the establishment of the California State Park Commission. The need for a state park system and a sound state park and recreation policy was early clear to the directors and administrators of the Save-the-Redwoods League, for the simple reason that preservation of the redwood groves necessarily implied protection, which, in turn, called for efficient administration of the groves. This seemed then—and still seems to be—a proper state function.

But it was of major concern to the League because, having raised the money, bought the groves, and turned them over to the state, the League would suffer if any of the groves which it had helped to acquire were subsequently damaged through negligence or inadequate administrative protection.

As a result, the League's directors took an active interest in the creation of a state park commission to administer the lands already assigned for park purposes. Legislation to create such a commission was vetoed in 1927 by Governor Richardson. When reintroduced under Governor C. C. Young it was duly enacted. The League was in the fortunate position that one of its directors, Duncan McDuffie, was close to Governor Young and was often consulted by him on matters of conservation. It was certainly with McDuffie's approval, if not at his suggestion, that Governor Young named as chairman of the newly created State Park Commission Mr. William E. Colby, who, as I have mentioned earlier, was one of the original organizers and directors of the Save-the-Redwoods League. Mr. Colby held this post for nine years, and in his days the office had great influence. When the reorganization of the state governmental structure took place in 1956 the State Park Commission, like the State Recreation Commission, was relegated to an innocuous status.

Although the Save-the-Redwoods League had no official part in the selection of the men chosen by the State Park Commission to make a survey of the state's park and recreation resources which had been authorized by the State Legislature, it may be assumed that Chairman Colby discussed with his friends in the League the possibility and desirability of getting the then famous American landscape architect, Frederick Law Olmsted, Jr., to survey the state's park potentials and to detail a state park and recreation policy. Olmsted, like his famous father before him, was one of the nation's soundest students and planners in the field of parks and recreation. I am sure that the directors of the Save-the-Redwoods League noted with interest and satisfaction, among the conclusions in Olmsted's report on California's park problems, the one that read "to preserve adequate and worthy examples of virgin redwood forests is by far the most important and urgent single duty of the State Park Commission in relation to forest types." Here, clearly, was a man after their own hearts.

It is unfortunate that the revival of nation-wide interest in the establishment of a redwoods national park in 1967 and 1968 was accompanied by somewhat hysterical full-page ads in national newspapers, some of which gave the impression that the redwoods were on the verge of immediate and complete extinction. The truth is, of course, that few species of trees reproduce so bountifully as does the *sequoia sempervirens*. Not only do the Coast Redwoods seed profusely, but unlike most other trees, they put out new growth from cut stumps. Furthermore, the redwoods in their native habitat are luxurious and fast growers. I have seen stands of second-growth redwoods a hundred years old which anywhere else than in the redwood belt would be regarded as superb trees, although, of course, not even remotely resembling the old giants in size. Doubtless if we could wait till the year 3500 or 4000 A.D. and could prevent all cutting of redwoods until then, there would be plenty of redwoods of all sizes to satisfy the ideals of all but the most extreme conservationists.

All of which helps to point up the key fact that the aim of the preservationists is to save the relatively few remaining stands of the giants which are not yet protected, rather than to seek large segments of marketable timber. Although preservationists disagree as to how many giants are enough, most of them would probably be satisfied if the present acreage of giants now in state parks could be doubled, and their preservation made doubly sure. This would still leave the lumber industry about 90 per cent of the profitable marketable acreage of uncut redwoods, as well as large areas of denuded cut-over lands which, according to spokesmen for the industry, could be successfully replanted. While a theoretical argument can be made in behalf of preserving in their pristine condition some, at least, of the primitive redwoods younger than the giants, it should be borne in mind that most of the state park groves of redwood giants are surrounded by younger trees, which help to protect the giants from the elements. The main objective, I repeat, is to save as many as possible of the very large coast redwoods not yet in state parks.

Active experience in choosing and acquiring groves of redwoods during the last half century has convinced the staff of the Save-the-Redwoods League that areas to be protected neither can, nor should, be limited to a bare minimum acreage. They have also learned the value of acquiring watersheds above the groves. This is important because many of the groves of large trees are near stream beds or actually on the floors of canyons. They are thus exposed to damage by floods, particularly floods from recently cut-over watersheds, which often carry large logs of green timber. There are, of course, indisputable evidences of silting caused by prehistoric floods long before the arrival of white men in California. This fact is often used by spokesmen for the lumber industry as an argument against the claims of conservationists that watersheds above groves of giants must be kept uncut in order to prevent damage downstream by flooding. But it is illogical to contend that because old groves survived prehistoric floods it necessarily follows that groves downstream from recently cut-over watersheds have not been damaged by floods and will escape injury in the future. Men who have studied the effects of flooding on groves now in state parks are convinced that the prevention of cutting on watersheds above these groves is an essential part in the preservation of most of these groves of old redwood giants.

The enactment of a bill establishing a Redwood National Park came only after sharp disagreements as to areas to be included in the park. The bill as finally passed has been considered by various groups to be inadequate. Necessarily it did not include all of the areas that all of the conservationists wanted, but in behalf of the bill it should be pointed out that the mere establishment of a Redwood National Park has long been overdue. It is true that the California State Redwood Parks, which are now transferred to Federal jurisdiction, were well cared for and were safe from commercial destruction. But as indicated in Chapter XV, these state parks were not immune from the bulldozers of California's highway engineers.

As this is one of the few instances in which transfer of state park lands to the National Park Service is involved, technical details may be slow in being finally adjusted. Among the unusual factors in this particular case are the possible legal complexities that may arise from the fact that nearly all of the money raised by the Save-the-Redwoods League for the acquisition of fine stands of coast redwoods to be transferred to the California State Park System came from gifts. In many of these bequests, the idea of permanent maintenance as part of the California State Park system was stressed. Some of the donors already have sought information as to what might happen if any of the state lands transferred to the Federal government were to be either abandoned or used for nonpark purposes by the Federal government. Doubtless, in time, the legal points involved can be clarified so as to preclude misunderstandings.

Although the arguments in behalf of a National Park have, as I pointed out earlier in this chapter, long been clear, many persons concerned about saving redwoods are understandably distressed that the Redwood National Park bill, as enacted in 1968, has included only a small amount of fine old trees not previously protected. It is therefore to be hoped that additional stands of unprotected giants can and will be added to the National Park or to state parks before they are sacrificed to the lumber interests.

STORMING STORM KING

STORM KING is the most spectacular mountain in the Hudson River Highlands, fifty miles north of Manhattan. Although it is a dwarf compared to many mountains in the West, its setting makes it look like a giant.

As late as 1960 Storm King seemed safe for the ages. It is too steep to be suburbanized or industrialized. Although rumors spread in the late 1950s that some of the more nostalgic purveyors of electric power to New York City were toying with harnassing the Hudson and might want to build a hydroelectric power plant at Storm King, yet the development of new sources of power throughout the nation pointed to cheaper and more efficient ways of generating electricity than by water—except in such rare areas as Niagara Falls.

But on January 19, 1963, Consolidated Edison (Con Ed) applied to the Federal Power Commission (FPC) for a license to install a big hydroelectric plant at Storm King, to be run by pumping water from the Hudson up to the top of the mountain, where it would be held in a huge reservoir and released through a tunnel forty feet in diameter to operate turbine generators just above the high-water level of the Hudson. So fantastic was the scheme in this age of jet propulsion and nuclear power that few took Con Ed seriously. The proposal seemed like suggesting the reintroduction of coal-burning elevated railways to relieve Manhattan's transit troubles in the last third of the twentieth century. As the details of Con Ed's proposal leaked out, incredulity increased. When it was learned that three kilowatts of power would be needed to pump enough water to the mountain reservoir to produce two kilowatts when released through the turbine generators, some of the Hudson River Highlanders quoted to each other the words of a once famous neighbor of theirs, spoken in another context: "Who's loony now?" Not until they learned that the village of Cornwall had agreed to sell a major source of its fresh water supply to Con Ed—part of which watershed was a recent gift to the town for the purpose of insuring a permanent water supply for Cornwall—did the opponents of the project begin to realize that a desperately serious threat to the Hudson River Valley existed. "We had all been asleep at the switch," was the way one of them explained to me their reaction to Con Ed's plan.

As has happened in other cases, a number of outraged local residents banded together to try to save the area which they loved. While space does not permit listing those who opposed the Storm King project from the beginning, various members have told me that they were only loosely organized at the start, and were handicapped by the fact that most of them had had little experience in the difficult technique of fighting a powerful public utility corporation which had many political supporters and almost unlimited funds to spend for publicity. But as has been pointed out in other chapters, it is still possible for a relatively small group of determined citizens to arouse public opinion in behalf of a good cause.

Most of the details of the hearing about the Storm King project before the FPC are of interest primarily to engineers. To conservationists the importance of the case lies in the fact that Con Ed prevailed and was granted a license by the FPC; that Con Ed's opponents, banded together as the Scenic Hudson Preservation Conference, petitioned the United States Court of Appeals to have the action of the FPC reconsidered; that the Court of Appeals by unanimous decision remanded the case to the FPC and directed that agency, in reconsidering the application, to include "as a basic concept the preservation of natural beauty and of national historic shrines, keeping in mind that in our opulent society the cost of a project is only one of several factors to be considered"; and that when Con Ed petitioned the Supreme Court of the United States to review the action of the Court of Appeals, the Supreme Court declined to do so.

The support of most of the nation's leading conservation societies, both before and after the FPC hearings, was a great help to the Scenic Hudson Preservation Conference. Among them were the National Audubon Society, the Nature Conservancy, the Isaak Walton League, the Sierra Club, the National Parks Association, the Garden Club of America, the Wilderness Society, and many other groups. The case was typical of the kind of threat that is ever present so long as self-styled apostles of progress see a chance to make money by defacing scenery. The outcome was convincing evidence that advances in the progress of conservation do not just happen. They are the result of alertness, ingenuity, persistence, and influence—using this last word to mean good publicity and access to officials who can help guide government intervention—and it should be borne in mind that conservation projects of all kinds are largely dependent on the approval, and often active cooperation, of one or more levels of government. This presents complications—and often leads to conflict—because of the separation of powers which characterizes the American form of government: separation of powers not only between the executive, legislative, and judicial branches, but also by geographical factors. Many persons think of "government" as a sort of unitary organization, whereas, in fact, government in the United States is divided into compartments and bureaus. Furthermore, there is little intercommunication between the different levels of government—national, state, and local—even when bureaus of the different levels are striving toward the same or similar goals. In some cases initiative lies in a county or subdivision, in others in the state, and in still others in the Federal government, and this initiative has to be sparked, or at least encouraged. Common sense cooperation between different levels of government cannot be taken for granted, even though the press usually rides herd on various levels of government, and sometimes can force attention on common problems.

In the Storm King case the initial decision rested in a Federal body—the Federal Power Commission—whose function is to pass on the licensing of power projects of more than purely local concern. This commission holds public hearings, at which opponents of a particular project may be heard after an applicant has outlined in detail the project for which he seeks a license.

The local opponents of the Storm King project who spoke at the hearings before the FPC against Con Ed's application realized that in Con Ed they faced one of the most powerful corporations in the country, with long experience in winning

and holding political support. They also knew that as opponents of Con Ed they would have to win the support of commission members who neither knew nor cared about conservation and who were accustomed to considering applications
for licenses solely on technical engineering grounds. About
the only means within reach of Con Ed's opponents was to
stir up public opinion against the project.

To the members of the Scenic Hudson Preservation Conference the task seemed hard indeed. As one of them wrote
me: "We knew nothing at the start about the 'how' of conservation and had merely contributed to conservation causes
elsewhere, letting others do the work. We had taken our own
scenic heritage for granted and thought that conservationists
were people who saved redwoods, dinosaurs, swans, and
swamps. And I may add that our experience turned a lot of
us into conservationists." Judging by results, newly converted
conservationists can be very effective. This group early em-
ployed the service of an experienced publicity man to bring
their cause to the attention of the public, and when the FPC
granted Con Ed its license to build the Storm King project,
these conservation neophytes not only decided to petition the
United States Court of Appeals for a reconsideration of the
FPC's decision, but they had the good judgment to pick as
their legal counsel for this task, one of the nation's most distinguished lawyers—Lloyd K. Garrison, former dean of the
University of Wisconsin's law school. Few attorneys are his
equal in intellect and character. Together with his heritage
of a strong sense of social responsibility from his forebear,
William Lloyd Garrison of abolitionist fame, he has an advo-
cate's mastery of clear analysis, together with the drive of a
crusader and the zeal of a convert. (He wrote me that he knew

little about the conservation movement before he took up this case, but that now he was "intensely interested" in it.)

His summing up of Scenic Hudson's plea to the Court of Appeals for a rehearing by the FPC, on the grounds that that commission had failed to explore thoroughly the serious flaws inherent in the project, was so comprehensive as to be incontrovertible. These perils included the dangers to fish life resulting from pumping vast amounts of water out of the river (it so happens that in this part of the Hudson, salt water fish, particularly striped bass, have their spawning grounds and that the eggs and young fish would be vulnerable to destruction by fish screens and turbines); the danger to inland water sources and plant life from the seepage of saline Hudson River water from the reservoir behind the mountain; the danger to people and property below the dam site from accidental flooding; and most important in the eyes of conservationists, the danger to scenic beauty. He stressed that overhead transmission lines through Putnam County, which are an integral part of the project, would cause extensive economic injury to nearby property owners. He also elaborated the fact that evidence of the availability of feasible alternatives to the Storm King project had not been sufficiently covered in the hearings before the FPC and that the public interest is so great that the commission had a duty to receive relevant evidence regarding possible alternatives even though offered after the initial hearings had been closed. He also contended that the FPC had erred in finding that the Con Ed project was "best adapted" to a "comprehensive plan to improve and develop a waterway" as required by the Federal Power Act. In conclusion he stated that the commission failed to weigh together, and to give adequate weight to, all the factors required by the Act. He therefore asked that the case be reopened in order that consideration might be given to grave policy questions of all kinds, including the relation of the Federal authorities with the state and municipalities.

The fact that the court of appeals unanimously sustained Mr. Garrison's plea and remanded the case to the FPC did not, of course, mean that the Storm King project was, *ipso facto*, defeated. But the decision assured a further examination of all factors in the case, and its comprehensiveness suggests that it will have major importance in the development of judicial support of conservation projects of all kinds in the future. To a layman the court's insistence that the conservation of scenic values should be carefully weighed against purely economic factors stands out as of particular significance.

It is interesting that after the decision by the Court of Appeals *The New York Times* editorially questioned the capacity of the FPC to make broad, rather than merely technical, decisions. In an editorial of about the same date in the *Herald-Tribune,* the pertinent observation was made that the FPC as well as Consolidated Edison "ought to realize that the public interest cannot be secured in kilowatts alone." Clearly opinion was beginning to emphasize the protection of scenic resources for the long-range benefit of the public.

Fortunately, while the legal aspects of the project were receiving fresh consideration, important political developments arose. Governor Rockefeller at first favored the Con Ed project. In reply to Assemblyman A. Watson Pomeroy, of Dutchess County, chairman of the Joint Legislative Committee on Natural Resources, who wrote to the Governor asking him to request a delay in the handing down of the FPC decision, the Governor wrote: "On balance, in my judgment, the values of this project—with proper safeguards for the aesthet-

ics during and after construction and with consideration for
the importance of the large amount of jobs to be provided
for the area during the construction—outweigh the objections which have been raised to it."

The Governor's endorsement of Con Ed's plan brought
sharp criticism from the press. The New York *Herald-
Tribune* described the Governor's position as "a disappoint-
ment," and ended by saying that "the plain fact is that neither
Con Ed nor the Governor has shown why the Storm King ven-
ture, incapable of correction when done, is so essential." *The
New York Times* characterized the Governor's position as
showing "a shocking departure from all that the governor's
family has stood for over the years in the fight to preserve natural beauty and historic sites. It is hard to believe that the
son of a man who saved the Palisades and the Jackson Hole
country in Wyoming, and who restored Williamsburg, could
approve the spoliation of the Hudson Highlands." A local
newspaper, the *Peekskill Evening Star,* described the Governor's endorsement of Con Ed's project as "a bitter blow to
the thousands of area residents who have opposed the project,
not to mention conservationists and others who fear further
spoliation of the Hudson River's scenic beauty."

In retrospect it is surprising that few, if any, of the com-
mentators pointed out that the Governor's acceptance of the
idea that the project would bring added employment opportunities for local residents showed either marked disingenu-
ousness or a facile disregard of the fact that a large amount
of the work—notably, tunneling, specialized masonry, and the
installation of massive but delicate machinery—required exceptional skills and long experience and thus would be performed in large part by imported, highly trained laborers.
It is true that outsiders brought in as temporary residents of

the area would spend money at local stores. But the likelihood of greatly increased local employment due to the project was and is largely illusory.

Apparently with an eye to counteracting this criticism, the Governor on March 26, 1965, announced the appointment of a so-called Hudson River Valley Commission to study the problems of the preservation of the valley. He explained that this commission should consider "a wide range of concerns: recreational, industrial, historic, scenic, commercial, cultural, residential and aesthetic." He went on to say that "in this day of advancing technology, expanding population, urbanization and rising standards of living, it is vital that we plan to preserve and intelligently use our precious natural resources, in order that our society may grow and prosper, not only materially but in an environment rich in natural beauty, historic ties and aesthetic values as well." He stated that the commission's "guide lines and recommendations for action will relate to the entire length of the Hudson and will cover administrative and legislative action at all levels of government." To this commission the Governor appointed his brother, Laurance S. Rockefeller, W. Averill Harriman, Mrs. Marion Sulzberger Heiskell, Lowell Thomas, William H. Whyte, Jr., and a number of others.

On June 28, 1965, the New York legislature enacted the Hudson River Corridor Act, which stated, among other things, that "the legislature . . . finds and declares that steps should be initiated to assure the orderly protection and use of this river area which is so intimately related to the heritage of this state, the variety of its greatness and the fullness of its future." The Act directed the Hudson River Valley Commission to "make a detailed land-use analysis, including a survey of the scenic, historic and cultural resources of the

Hudson River Valley area," and to recommend to the governor and the legislature "steps to protect and enhance" these resources. At the same time the legislature authorized the issue of $200,000,000 of bonds for the acquisition of "parks, forest recreation areas, marine facilities and historic sites" subject to approval by a referendum. This approval was given in the November election.

On February 1, 1966, the Hudson River Valley Commission issued a summary report to the Governor, urging the necessity of an interstate protection plan for the entire valley, recommending the appointment of a permanent commission, to include representatives of the Federal government and of the states of New York and New Jersey, and local governments for a concerted effort to guide the future growth of the valley. With regard to the Storm King project the report said: "The commission believes that scenic values are paramount here and that the plant should not be built here if a feasible alternative can be found." It went on to recommend that "if an alternative is found the Storm King site should be acquired by the State as park land and that other sites now under consideration for pump storage plants in the Highlands area be similarly acquired."

A few months after the publication of this report the New York legislature enacted (May 11, 1966) the Hudson River Valley Commission Act which set up a permanent commission and which provided for coordinated long-range planning and action to "preserve, enhance and develop" the resources of the area. This Act broadened the powers of the earlier Hudson River Valley Corridor Act and enlarged the jurisdiction of the commission to include lands visible from the river within two miles of its shore.

In the meantime Congress became interested in saving the

Hudson, and on September 16, 1966, it enacted a bill creating an interstate compact between New York, New Jersey, and the Federal government for the preservation and development of the Hudson River. Among other things this act included a declaration to the effect that "the Hudson River basin contains resources of immense economic, natural, scenic, historic and recreation values for all the citizens of the United States," thus indicating that the future of the Hudson River was of national concern.

The Federal act then stated: "It is the sense of the Congress that Federal departments and agencies should, insofar as possible, consider the effects of projects or actions upon achievement of the objectives of this act until the compact has been acted upon by the states and the Federal government." It also included the provision that the Secretary of the Interior should represent the United States in consulting with the heads of Federal agencies. By indirection this implied that the Secretary would be empowered to at least advise on any action by a commission such as the FPC, which seemed to be running counter to the intent of Congress as expressed in this Act.

As a result of these political and legal activities the chances are that the Storm King case will long be "unfinished business." The hearings directed by the U. S. Court of Appeals were held before the FPC's trial examiner beginning in November 1966, running daily with a break at Christmas until around the middle of May 1967. By the end of 1967 it appeared that unless the commission itself should conclude that the voluminous record thus made before the trial examiner contained gaps, there would be no further hearings before the commission. Judging from the mass of material presented to the trial examiner it would probably take him months to prepare and render his report. This report would go before the commission and at that time further briefs and oral examinations could be considered. Judging by the slow rate of progress usual in such cases, the chances are that no decision would be reached within six to ten months after the hearings, and that the loser would probably appeal to the United States Court of Appeals, with the possibility that the case might even go before the Supreme Court of the United States.

There is, of course, no way of foretelling how long these moves might take, or what the higher courts might decide. But the case shows clearly that the fervent dedication of a determined group of private citizens in a sound cause can accomplish much. Had there been no Scenic Hudson Preservation Conference, Con Ed would have begun despoiling Storm King in 1964 or 1965. So long as the case remains unconcluded every month's delay increases the likelihood that the power company will decide that other methods of producing electricity will prove to be cheaper and more efficient than the Storm King project and that, in consequence, Con Ed, as an act of enlightened self-interest, will abandon this proposal. To date the cause of conservation throughout the nation has acquired new status, thanks to judicial re-emphasis on scenic values as a part of the nation's heritage.

A COUNTY SAVES A COAST

For a hundred miles south from the Monterey peninsula, the dome-shaped headlands of California's rugged Coast Range rise out of the rock-shored Pacific to a height of four to five thousand feet. The ocean side of the range has heavy rains in winter, often turning to snow near the crest. In the northern half of the area redwoods crowd its short, steep canyons, watered by cold streams lined with ferns and moss. Steelhead come up from the sea to spawn. Deer browse in the brush. Sickle-billed thrashers perched on the dry tops of old *ceanothus* bushes pour out long songs of thanks for each sparkling day. Red-tailed hawks ride as if at anchor in the updraft of the trade winds, ready to plummet down to snatch a pack rat. Still higher, eagles sometimes soar above the mountain crest. On the ridges are ponderosa and Coulter pines, madrone, Lucia firs and tanbark oaks and, at lower levels, live oaks and sycamores. Dominating the scenery is the sea, blue as the Mediterranean when clear, but often deep in fog. On quiet nights the fog engulfs the hills, but by midmorning the northwest trades disperse it, sheeting the ocean with whitecaps.

In the early 1920s this part of the coast was roadless. Trails were tough on mules and men and rarely used by strangers. The area's few ranchers gloried in their isolation and were self-sufficient, making only one or two trips a year across the rugged crest to King City, or up the coast to Monterey. They loved their steep mountainside with a passion strange to men who live on plains or even in the hills of New England, and utterly unknown to city dwellers. The cool sea air brought them health and strength. Each autumn they prayed for early rains to end the threat of fire that could blast a mountainside in minutes in the rainless summer and autumn, bringing death to all living things.

But this remote wilderness was not to remain cut off forever. At great cost, the California Division of Highways in the 1920s and 1930s blasted the coast road around the mountains' rocky headlands, spanning deep canyons with tall bridges made of redwoods. It was a two-lane road with sharp curves high above the ocean, not meant for speed or heavy traffic, but, rather, a scenic drive along a rugged coast. To build it called for skill and ingenuity.

In the center of this coastal strip is what has long been spoken of as "The Big Sur country." (The name is half-English and half-Spanish. In New Mexico they would say: "Rio Grande del Sur," and in New England, "Big South River.") The strip extends along seventy-two miles of coast and mountains and had in the census of 1960 a population of 659.

My first visit to Big Sur was in 1928, before the coast road had been finished beyond the Big Sur valley. I drove a secondhand Ford from Monterey to what is known as Post's Summit, about two miles south of the Pfeiffer Big Sur State

Park. There Bill Post furnished me with a saddle horse and pack horse, and I spent a week riding down the coast past Slate's Hot Springs to Gamboa's ranch and back over the old coast trail. It was early in May, and the grass-covered promontories between the wooded canyons were thick with orange-yellow California poppies, blue-and-white annual lupins, and raspberry-colored owl's clover, all in full bloom. Little did I suspect that within ten years I would own property on the coast and after World War II would make my home in Big Sur and in due time would join a group of Big Sur residents to help launch what is now known as "The Monterey County Coast Master Plan," which was an important contribution to the extension of county zoning and control in fields of conservation.

Credit is usually given to the late Dr. John L. D. Roberts for having initially suggested the building of a scenic road along the coast. This was in the 1890s. Construction did not start until the 1920s. To a Monterey lawyer, Carmel Martin, belongs the honor of having persuaded the Monterey County Board of Supervisors, of which he was then a member, to ban billboards along the new road as it was pushed down the coast in those early days, one of the first—and few—times that a county dared defy the billboard industry. The same Carmel Martin was chairman of the Monterey Coast Highway Study Commission appointed in 1957 by the Monterey County Planning Commission to consider and report on the future of the Coast Highway. As I also was named a member of this highway study commission, I saw much of Martin throughout its deliberations. Our recommendations foreshadowed some of the controls that were ultimately incorporated in the Master Plan.

The future of the Big Sur country was not seriously

threatened until 1959 and 1960. Our first warning came from friends who worked on the highway maintenance crew who told us that the engineers in the division of highways planned to use dirt fills to replace some of the tall redwood bridges that straddled the deep canyons. In retrospect, it sounds innocuous, but those of us familiar with the country knew that to make fills, some of which would have to be enormous, the engineers would have to blast and bulldoze masses of material for hundreds of feet above the highway, and the resulting scars would be as ugly as they would be enduring. The lovely canyons containing redwoods, ferns, and streams would be badly marred by these ugly fills so alien to the area. We also suspected that if the engineers planned to replace two-lane bridges with huge fills, they must be looking ahead to the ultimate widening and straightening of the road—which would do irreparable damage to this superb country.

When we first queried the engineers, they gave us the usual polite bureaucratic brushoff. But when they learned that one of our group, the architect Nathaniel A. Owings of the firm of Skidmore, Owings and Merrill, knew much about bridge building, they suggested that he bring two other local residents to meet with the engineers in Monterey to be briefed about their plans. Accordingly Owings, together with Harry-dick Ross, who for thirty years had hiked all over the coast range and fought forest fires in it, and I (then chairman of the Big Sur Advisory Committee of the Monterey County Planning Commission) met with the engineers. They were polite but reserved, even when Owings talked knowingly of the number of truck loads of fill to be dumped into the canyons, and the relative cost of replacing redwood bridges with concrete bridges. My role was to listen, and the more I heard the madder I got as it became clear that the engineers just couldn't care less about what residents thought of the road builders defacing the country. They had been indoctrinated by the state director of public works, who is quoted as having said that "the people of California, through the Department of Public Works, have placed responsibility for the adequacy *or inadequacy* of the design and construction of any state highway on the Division of Highways." Translated into plain English this was a new form of the old phrase: "Momma knows best!" The division's plans could not be questioned and would not be changed. While the division's record shows that it has a sense of responsibility, the implication was clear that if something which it planned to do was sound engineering, it was beyond discussion—let alone modification—even though it might injure the beauty of the coast. Their attitude was that of Commodore Vanderbilt, famous builder of railroads a century ago, who, when told that the public would not like something that his engineers planned to do, coined the famous phrase: "The public be damned!"

When I joined my wife for lunch on the wharf at Monterey right after the meeting with the highway engineers she listened to my report and asked tartly: "Why don't you do something about it?" To my query: "What can I do?" she replied: "Order yourself a drink and then call up Ed Kennedy at the *Monterey Peninsula Herald*." This I did, and Ed, who was one of the nation's ablest journalists, suggested that I call his office when I had finished lunch. He asked keen questions about the situation and then said: "How soon could you do a series of articles for us?" I named a date, and the *Herald* published the articles—five of them. Local response was good, and the engineers, already under severe criticism from the *Herald* for the routing of a throughway into Monterey, could not ignore it.

As I look back through my scrapbooks and files, I see that many things worked in our favor. Our goals were limited—to save from two threats this area of the California coast which had only a few hundred residents. The first threat came from the highway engineers, whose ultimate aim was (and still is) to straighten out and widen the road, and the second came from real-estate developers who hoped to buy up and subdivide the land along the highway. Fortunately, the two groups had little in common. The engineers were interested only in moving traffic and looked on this coast road as a link in their main north-south arteries. The real-estate developers' sole concern was to sell as many lots as possible along the highway for the highest prices that they could get, and then move on to other potential developments. Both groups looked on a master plan to preserve this area as an unwarranted and intolerable affront to their freedom of action.

Of the two groups, the division of highways presented the most immediate threat, as changes in the road would leave scars which time could not heal. But it was our good luck that the division of highways had many enemies throughout the state, and that in Sacramento many politicians had feuded with the engineers. Fortunately, Monterey County's representative in the state senate, Fred S. Farr, was deeply interested in conservation and had friendly ties with those of us who wanted to see the coast saved "as is." Not only did he know what we might be able to do but how we could best do it. His advice proved invaluable. We were also fortunate in that the Monterey County Board of Supervisors was at that time, as it had long been, made up of able, public-spirited citizens who were proud that the board's record through the decades was one of the most enlightened of the nation's three thousand county governments. They knew the value to the county of preserving the coast area from unwise exploitation, and in the person of Thomson J. Hudson, its member from the Monterey-Carmel area, our group was assured of effective contacts as the movement developed. Furthermore, my next-door neighbor, Keith B. Evans, former mayor of Carmel, was a highly respected member of the Monterey County Planning Commission. As director of the technical staff of that commission was Mr. Ed DeMars, an able and devoted official whose work in all phases of conservation in the county has been effective and constructive for years.

I go into these details because they point up the value of personal contacts in matters involving cooperation between county officials and interested private citizens. The initial impetus may come from voters, but most of the work in the preparation and development of any such project as a master plan, or even a new zoning ordinance, is done by able technicians on the county staff. Our task was made easier by the fact that the county of Monterey early in 1960 accepted an offer from the architectural and engineering firm of Skidmore, Owings and Merrill to prepare a master plan for the scenic coast. As Mr. Owings had recently built a home at Big Sur, and as he and his wife (who later was for years a member of the California State Park Commission) played a major part in organizing support for a master plan on the part of the coast residents, this association proved productive. Those of us who helped develop the plan had sound advice from professional planners of world-wide experience, and the county technicians had access to experts in this kind of work.

The master plan, as drawn up by Skidmore, Owings and Merrill, was presented to the County Planning Commission in October 1960. It combined protection of the coast's spectacular scenery with zoning expressly designed to avoid unjustifiable restrictions and hardships on present and future property owners. The proposed zoning regulations called for: (1) density control of real-estate developments, including the clustering of houses with the express purpose of leaving a large proportion of the land permanently in open space; (2) design control and landscaping; (3) prevention of soil erosion; and (4) measures to avoid ill-planned private road building. The report also recommended that the coast highway be designated by state law as a "scenic road" for leisurely travel by vacationists and tourists, rather than as a throughway dedicated to speed.

Looking back on the project, it is interesting to read, on the opening page of what was technically called "The Short Form Report," the postulate that "basically the problem is one of conservation, which cannot be solved by the traditional procedure of making the area into a state or national park." The report stated that what was needed was "a new device for the conservation of scenic resources within a specified area, with the proviso that when and if changes in the use of privately owned lands are projected, such changes shall be subject to review by the County Planning Commission." It suggested that the county take the lead in establishing a type of conservation area to be known as a "scenic reserve" and explained that within such an area "existing range and agricultural uses would be unconditional, but new zoning regulations as described in the master plan would not only provide for density control but also for design control and landscaping, as well as for measures for preventing erosion and unwise road building." It further declared that "Highway #1 is a scenic road and should be recognized as such by the county and the state," and suggested that scenic roads should be defined by statute as "leisurely travel lanes for vacationists and tourists, rather than as arterials dedicated to speed." It recommended that the division of highways should not only be empowered but also directed to recognize this new category of roads "and to preserve the natural beauties of areas through which scenic roads pass." With reference to the coast highway, it urged that there be no drastic realignment of the roadbed and opposed replacing bridges with fills. Under the heading "A Ribbon of Open Country" it recommended that the land adjacent to the road should.be kept as free as possible from residential or commercial developments where these would mar the scenic values of the area. It suggested classifying the land in the area in three sections: "(a) the shore belt, comprising land between the highway and the ocean; (b) the meander line belt, comprising land between the highway and the set-back or meander line of varying depth to the east of the highway; and, (c) the mountain or range belt consisting of land between the meander line and the crest of the mountains, or the boundary of the National Forests." First in the order of importance it listed keeping the belt of land between the highway and the ocean in its present unbuilt condition. As second objective, it named the need to hold construction to a minimum between the highway and the meander line. In both of these belts, it recommended a basic density control of ten acres to each homesite.

Particularly important was the recommendation that "a new density standard should be applied in which the primary emphasis is on creating and preserving open space." In so doing, the plan advocated following the proposed "clustering principle," which as recently as 1960 was regarded as novel and even revolutionary. In summary, the report stated that "part of the creation of a new category of highways to be known as 'scenic roads' would be a new emphasis on the importance of conservation of the scenic resources adjacent to the road."

The Owings plan, as it came to be called, met with fierce opposition from a group of real-estate operators who wanted to acquire as much land as possible along the highway and then subdivide. Except for deliberate misrepresentations in the efforts to block the plan, they based their opposition on the same grounds as have all realtors and developers elsewhere—rigid rejection of any form of zoning or of restricting the right of a seller to fragment his property into the smallest possible salable lots. The real-estate developers, eager to defeat the Monterey Coast Master Plan (of whom the most virulent was not even a resident of Monterey County), received support primarily from old-time ranchers whose hopes of being able to sell small parts of their land at good prices naturally made them distrustful of zoning and of all efforts to restrict the ratio of houses to acreage.

Fully as interesting as the contents of the Owings plan was the fact that its supporters made every effort possible to familiarize local residents with the details of the plan as they were worked out. Discussion was encouraged, and every effort was made to explain how the plan was expected to work. Objections and modifications were welcomed. To no one's surprise the local community was divided. Old feuds took on new luster, and the nonresident real-estate operators who sought to block the master plan tried to intensify hard feelings by spreading false rumors, such as that Owings had bought up all the land in the area and that henceforth no one could buy without Owings' consent. Few took the charges too seriously—including those who made them—but they served to make rational discussion of problems of widespread community concern difficult.

This, too, unexpectedly played into our hands, as it meant that the details, instead of being threshed out locally, would have to be discussed at meetings of the Monterey County Planning Commission in Salinas, a hundred-mile round trip from Big Sur. The Planning Commission was composed of high-minded, public-spirited citizens, who had no personal interests for or against our plan. The commission's technical staff was familiar with all the details of the Owings plan as presented and had suggested helpful modifications in the plan which strengthened it. The influence of Senator Farr and of Tom Hudson with the Planning Commission was also helpful, with the result that when details of the plan were presented, they had a fair hearing where it was most needed— from the men and women whose duty was to formulate the county's policy and recommend action to the Board of Supervisors.

In the final meetings in Salinas, each side presented its case fully with only occasional vehemence. As I had for years been appearing before the Planning Commission in my capacity of chairman of the Big Sur Advisory Committee, Mr. Owings and his legal counsel turned over to me a good deal of the work of clarifying nontechnical aspects of the Master Plan together with the more difficult task of summing up our case just before the commission was to vote on it. Armed only with notes, where ordinarily I spoke from a typed script, I started at the final meeting by expressing our belief in the value of the plan to the county and summed up the details. As I approached the end of the summary, I glanced at my notes (which I still have) and read: "Probably last appearance before the Commission." With a touch of mischievousness I looked up, paused for a moment to gain emphasis, and said that I had a strong feeling that this was probably the last time that I would address the commission (which, in fact, it was); whereupon, to my delight, the members of the opposition, who through all the hearings had sat together in a group across the aisle from us in the supervisors' chambers, clapped loudly and enthusiastically, and it suddenly dawned on me that they were expressing their relief and pleasure that they would never again have to hear me talk. When I realized that, quite unintentionally and unconsciously, they were paying tribute to the effectiveness of what I had said at previous meetings, it was hard for me to keep a straight face. I remember clasping my hands together and waving them above my head in the traditional gesture of victory. The chairman polled the board. The vote was four to three in our favor.

It is a measure of the importance of the Monterey County Coast Master Plan that the weekly magazine *Time* devoted a full page to its final passage (*Time,* December 28, 1962). In a sense it was a "natural." As *Time* summed it up the planners proposed:

> The drafting of zoning laws to limit the number of new houses and encourage their clustering—for example, ten houses with a hundred acres of land among them might be clustered on ten acres, leaving the remaining 90 acres clear.
>
> Acceptance of the principle that the view from the road is paramount, and new houses should be sited so that their roofs would not break the skyline.
>
> Limiting the coastal highway to the present two-lane width, with a 100-foot setback along its whole length.

The controlled expansion of tourist facilities, with the development of beaches and the building of at least two new harbors.

From the point of view of professional planners and of conservationists the score, on balance, was good. The Division of Highways dropped its plan to replace bridges with fills (but prudently completed the construction of freeways to the northern and southern ends of the coast road). The significance of this lies in the fact that a succession of California highway engineers, whenever they look at a map of the state's freeways, will be reminded that the inclusion of the coast road in the freeway system is a matter of "unfinished business" and will find it hard to resist trying to have the road widened and realigned.

Fortunately, the fact that this part of the coast highway was later officially declared by act of the legislature to be the first in a new type of road to be designated as a pilot project for "scenic roads" will make it more difficult for the engineers to widen it or change its alignment. As more roads are officially classed as "scenic roads," the division of highways may well find interesting precedents in this coast highway which may be useful in the development of engineering standards for the new category of scenic roads.

The aspect of the master plan which, as I have reviewed what was done, strikes me as most interesting is the one sometimes referred to as the concept of the "scenic corridor," to which, in mountainous terrain, is tied the concept of the "meander line." Both are necessarily variable, based on the geographical relation between the location of a scenic road and the land immediately adjoining it. Definitions are hard to find, but the idea of a scenic corridor seems the simpler and more obvious of the two. It suggests that on both sides of a scenic road there is—or should be—a ribbon of land of varying width from which, wherever possible, buildings, roadside stands, and billboards should be permanently excluded and artificial landscaping held to a minimum. Insofar as there are, or should be, standards, it has been suggested that wherever safety permits, as much as possible of the ribbon should be left in its natural state.

The term "meander line" is used to designate the uphill boundaries of a belt of land adjoining a scenic road, which is of varying width, determined primarily by its visibility from the road. The meander line is an arbitrary boundary, largely delineated by the lay of the land, and having as its function to designate the upper limit of an area along a scenic road within which specific restrictions as to building apply.

The concept of creating a "scenic reserve" which, in its simplest form, would be an area within which all current land uses would continue without restrictions, but changes in uses would have to have county approval, was apparently too logical to have much, if any, appeal. The objective was to "freeze" current uses (and nonuses) without surrendering to government the title to the property within an area so designated. The concept deserves further consideration, but when we presented it to experts in these fields, their reaction was that to implement the idea legally would be more difficult than to use the then relatively novel device of scenic easements. I mention it here because it is conceivable that it could be so shaped as to provide legal machinery for preserving lands permanently in their present condition without their being incorporated into a government-owned unit. Success in the development of the use of scenic easements has been so striking during the years that have passed since this suggestion of "scenic reserves" was considered that the concept no longer has much appeal.

Although a decade is a brief time in the life of any conservation device, I think that it can be said without fear of contradiction that the Monterey County Coast Master Plan was a major victory of the conservation movement at the local level. I use this extravagant characterization because the plan stands out as proof that when a group of citizens unite in a campaign to achieve a really important goal at the local level, they can attain noteworthy success.

WHAT LIES AHEAD

THE cause of conservation has prospered since the early 1900s—the inclusion of fine areas in National Parks and Monuments, the carefully controlled long-range development of resources of the National Forests, the creation of Wilderness Areas (even though with possibly inadequate protective clauses), definite advances in the protection of wildlife, and the setting aside of many state, county, and local parks and recreation areas in pleasant surroundings. Some of this dates back to the early days when no one knew much about conservation, and opposition to suggested restrictions on the use of natural resources was strong. We forget that the few outspoken advocates of saving scenery in the early decades were derided by self-styled conservationists as "preservationists"—a label intended to belittle and discredit them in a society which measured success in terms of quick consumption of the nation's natural resources. The implication was clear—that merely to preserve "as is" was foolish.

Today preservation dominates the thinking of conservationists: the saving of scenery and open space, the establishment of wilderness areas, new interest in wildlife sanctuaries. We now know that preservation need not imply nonuse, but that it does mean nonconsumption. It seeks to prevent mutilation of the environment for private gain, so that future Americans can enjoy what remains of the nation's scenic heritage. Particularly noteworthy is the fact that the enjoyment of environment does not involve consumption, as, for example, water in a lake used for swimming, fishing, and even motorboating, and trails for hiking which neither harm the environment nor consume resources. The motto of conservationists might well be: "Enjoy, but don't destroy."

The fact that outdoor recreation is now a major interest of millions of Americans has emphasized the value of scenery as a setting or backdrop for recreation. As Mr. Clifton E. French, director of the Hennepin County Park system in Minnesota, explained the relationship to me in the summer of 1968: "Parks are scenery; recreation is activity. The two belong together." Increased awareness of the beauty of environment is, in fact, as natural a by-product of the conservation movement since World War II as was concern with utilitarian values in the early 1900s a by-product of the materialistic thinking in that era. Conservationists in the early days feared exhaustion of consumable natural resources. Today they dread the destruction of natural beauty and open space.

Despite significant victories for conservation in the 1950s and 1960s, the war is not yet won. It seems sure that in the early 1970s and 1980s the supply of undeveloped land for almost any kind of use will be scant. The race for resources will force consumers of environment on lands already in their possession to speed up their bulldozers and sharpen their axes and saws before public opinion can be aroused to hold them in check. Particularly ominous are rumors that lumbermen are trying again to get access to timber in the National Parks and in the recently reserved Wilderness Areas in the National Forests from which they are presently excluded by law. (I use the phrase "presently excluded" advisedly because this exclusion was imposed by Congress, and what one Congress has enacted a succeeding Congress can change or repeal.)

The conservationists are handicapped by fighting for ideals against opponents who are fighting for profits. Furthermore, conservationists want to preserve, whereas their antagonists want to consume, and of the two processes consumption has the greater popular appeal. Of course conservation has keen supporters—more, now, than earlier. But the major decisions about conservation goals will be made by politicians, and in terms of practical politics the anticonservationists are powerful. Chief among them is the lumber industry and its subsidiaries and dependents. In second place are the nation's highway builders, backed by the manufacturers and suppliers of road-building equipment and materials, and by truck manufacturers and oil companies—a formidable group of business interests long served by skilled lobbyists. In addition there are the suburban real-estate developers throughout the nation, most of whom take a dim view of conservation, and are backed by local contractors, suppliers, and bankers. It may be generalized that almost any legislation which these groups want to see enacted will be hard to defeat. For decades they have fought the conservationists. Only the mining and grazing interests seem to be less aggressive now than they were in the days of Theodore Roosevelt, even though the coal miners have acquired the distinction which they did not have early in the century of having devised a method of operation

—strip mining—which is even more devastating to the environment than the lumbermen's activities in the last few decades.

Since the Civil War the lumber industry has cut—and grown fat on—almost all the reasonably accessible virgin timber on public lands within the continental United States. The industry's methods of harvesting timber are regarded by Europe's expert foresters as unbelievably—and inexcusably—wasteful and destructive. But when American laymen have expressed shock at the sight of cut-over lands in the redwoods country, industry spokesmen have tartly told them that no layman is capable of passing judgment on such a matter, that only a trained forester can understand that what looks like the site of a fierce battle in World War I or II—or a forerunner of atomic warfare—is a blessing in disguise. These spokesmen point with pride to seedlings taking root in bulldozed soil with plenty of sunlight, and indicate that these seedlings are lucky to be out of the dank, dark forests where the struggle for survival has been so hard on their kin that few trees have lived more than twenty centuries. Apparently professional lumbermen feel that what to a layman looks like desolation is the best thing that ever happened to the forest—or, at least, to the lumber industry.

On the "plus" side in the critical years ahead is the fact that although major policy decisions will be made, as in the past, at the political level, the administration of Federal and state parks, recreation areas, forests, and wildlife preserves will continue in the hands of experienced, dedicated men and women who have long held key positions in government bureaus. I have known many of them for years and have been struck with their ability and their devotion to the public interest. Furthermore, the increase in the number of semi-public organizations concerned with aspects of conservation, such as the Audubon Society, the Wilderness Society, the Sierra Club, and the Save-the-Redwoods League, has not only helped interest the public in various facets of conservation but also has produced a corps of watchers who make a business of keeping informed about the activities of the anticonservationists. Many conservation organizations collect and distribute informative and well-presented material which otherwise might escape the attention of conservationists.

It has been suggested that there should be a conservation clearinghouse. I question its utility for the reason that there are so many goals of conservation causes that they can best be helped by specialists. The causes are as varied as seeking more way stations for migratory waterfowl, saving redwoods, protecting sea otters, and seeking to preserve unscarred a particular part of a mountain range. Still other conservationists are interested primarily in procedural problems—the use of legal devices such as "open space," scenic easements, and clustering. Some want to see the inholdings in National Parks bought by the government. Others hope to see the Forest Service shift its emphasis from multiple use to nonconsumption.

Fortunately, along with these special causes, most of which are given effective help, there is a growing awareness that the time has come to challenge the claims of exploiters that they have the right to consume natural resources on public lands for their own profit. It should be clearly established and recognized that the national interest demands that these resources be protected from consumption and in particular, that the saving of scenery for the long-term enjoyment of present and future generations of Americans is more important to the nation as a whole than are the profits which the lumber companies hope to make in cutting the last stands of virgin timber in the National Forests which they can induce the Forest Service to let them cut. Why should conservationists accept unchallenged the concept that profits of lumber companies automatically take precedence over the interests of the nation as a whole? The mere fact that the lumber industry could profit handsomely if given access to virgin timber on public lands does not give the companies an inalienable right to be permitted to do so. The arguments of the thwarted consumers will have a familiar ring—that the nation is short of lumber, and that government has no right to lock up natural resources merely because crackpots want them saved for others to see. We shall be told that the dear God placed resources on this earth to be used, not just to serve as backdrops for frivolous activities such as outdoor recreation. Anyone familiar with the propaganda of opponents of conservation in the last few decades will recall other contentions of this sort which are as plausible as they are irrelevant.

It is here that the existing conservation organizations can be of particular help by joining in a campaign to publicize the fact to which I referred in the opening paragraph of this book—that scenery is in itself a natural resource. Stronger arguments can be made in behalf of preserving an area such as the North Cascade Range with its forests intact than can be made in behalf of permitting the lumber industry to strip this forest of its finest trees for their own profit. This area is an irreplaceable museum specimen of scenery. To permit the lumbermen to cut even only parts of its virgin timber would be a form of desecration and do irreparable damage.

If conservationists acquiesce in a revival of old attitudes

that private gain comes before all else, they will open the door to the ultimate destruction of many areas now under protection. Hetch Hetchy will become a sound precedent. Why not harness the Yellowstone geysers, and permit the cutting up of Yosemite's famous "Half Dome" for building blocks, and use the Yosemite Falls to generate electric power, and drain the Florida Everglades for a real-estate development? To the exploiters it is obviously intolerable to leave them as God made them.

Although now is the last chance to buy land for park and recreation purposes it must be noted that the mere transfer of title to land from a seller to a government bureau that is to have custody of it does not automatically assure permanent protection and wise use. As I have indicated, at least one set of officials at the Federal and state levels—the highway engineers—have been reckless and headstrong in unnecessary destruction of landscape. Furthermore, Congress, which set aside fine areas in National Parks with the express proviso that the natural resources within these areas are not to be opened to commercial exploitation, can reverse this policy at will.

The conclusion is inescapable: that conservation demands eternal vigilance—alertness to detect the schemes of its many enemies, and prompt steps to publicize the enemies' intentions. Conservation also calls for greater use of protective devices short of acquisition of title, such as zoning, open space, scenic and conservation easements, and "clustering." Fortunately, conservationists not only are vocal in behalf of particularly cherished causes but also generous in their support of others. Whether a conservationist's particular concern is saving redwoods, sea otters, condors, or wildflowers he (or she) is ready to ride and spread the alarm when other conservationists cry "Help!"—a cry that has often been heard since 1900 and is likely to be uttered frequently in the 1970s. Unless such cries are heeded promptly there will be little left to conserve.

INDEX

Agriculture, U. S. Department of, 6, 14, 16-20, 61
Albright, Horace M., 23, 24, 40-42, 44, 46-48, 56-58
American Forest Association, 4
Appalachian Park, 43
Asquam Lake Ski and Beach Club, N. H., 166-167
Astrup, Mark, 120-121, 122
Audubon Society, 4, 5, 166, 169, 199, 228
Ayres, Philip W., 158-159, 162

Barrett, Congressman (Wyo.), 58-59
Bass, Robert P., 158
Beauty, natural, protection of areas of, *see* Scenic areas, preservation of
Big Basin State Park, Calif., 186
"Big Sur country," Calif., 210-223
Biological Survey, U. S., 55, 151
Birds, 5
Boardman, Samuel H., 118
Boundary Waters Canoe Area, Minn., 78
Breaking New Ground (Pinchot), 14, 15

Bruns, Paul, 156-157
Bull Creek area, 4
Burt, Struthers, 57

California Resources Agency, 105
California State Park Commission, 191-192
California State Recreation Commission, 101, 192
Call of the Wild, The (London), 73
Cammerer, Arno B., 23
Cannon, "Uncle Joe," 160-161
Carey, Senator (Wyo.), 52
Carhart, Arthur, 77
Center Harbor, N. H., 167
Central Park, 181
Chateaubriand, Vicomte de, 73
Chessman, Merle, 119-120
Civil service, 13
Clark, William, 152-153
Classification and Multiple Use Act (1964), 99
Colby, William E., 29-31, 33, 37, 187, 192
Colorado River, 69
"Community Conservation Commissions," 165-166

233

Conservation and the Gospel of Efficiency (Hays), 100
Conservationists, types of, 5-6
Consolidated Edison, 197-204, 208
"Controlled uses," 17
Cooper, James Fenimore, 73
Court of Appeals, U. S., 199, 201-203, 207, 208
Cramton, Louis C., 49
Crocker, William H., 188

Dana, Charles A., 23
Darling, Jay N. ("Ding"), 150-152
Darling Foundation, 152
Defense, U. S. Department of, holdings of public lands by, 25
DeMars, Ed, 215
Deserts, 103-104
Dingell-Johnson Act, 146
Drury, Aubrey, 190-191
Drury, Newton B., 190-191
Ducks, 5, 150, 151
Darling's cartoon about, 151

Easements, 136-137, 142, 183, 222, 228, 230
Ecology, 27
Education, conservation, 6, 25, 85
Eleanor, Lake, 36
Elk, 55
Erosion, 4, 27, 64
"fuel breaks" and, 88
Evans, Keith B., 215
Everglades, 5, 230

Farr, Fred S., 176, 214, 219
Federal Power Act, 202
Federal Power Commission, 197, 199-203, 207
Fire fighting and prevention, 18, 70, 84-96
"Firebreaks," 88
Fish, 124-125, 202
Fisher, Sherry R., 152
Flood control, 64

Forest reserves, 16-20, 25
Forest Service, U. S., 6, 7, 14-21, 22, 24-25, 44, 55-56, 61-71, 97, 109, 115, 117, 121, 122, 127, 128, 228, 229
fire fighting activities, 84-96
wilderness areas and, 77-83
Forests, National, 18-21, 77, 79, 100, 112, 115, 127, 148, 159-162, 224, 226, 229
"multiple use" of, 64-71
Fosdick, Raymond B., 48
Franconia Notch, N. H., 163-165
French, Clifton E., 225
"Fuel breaks," 86, 87-88, 93

Garden Club of America, 199
Garfield, James R., 36, 99-100
Garrison, Lloyd K., 201-203
Garrison, William Lloyd, 201
General Land Office, 98-99
Geology, areas set aside as interesting samples of, 4
Gila National Forest, 77
Gila Wilderness Area, 77
Grand Canyon, 74, 153
Grand Teton National Park, 51-60, 153
Grant, Madison, 186, 187
Graves, Henry S., 162, 187
Grazing Service, 99
Grosvenor, Gilbert, 23

Hale, Lloyd, 131
Hancock, Mary Louise, 169
Hansen, William H., 85
Harriman, W. Averill, 205
Hays, Samuel P., 100
Heiskell, Mrs. Marion Sulzberger, 205
Hetch Hetchy Valley, 30-38, 75, 181, 230
Hirst, Edgar C., 158, 162-163
Historic Sites, National, 176
Historic Sites Commission, 176
Homestead Act (1862), 155

Homesteading, 18
Hood, Mount, 75
House Public Lands Committee, 52-59
Hudson, Thomson J., 215, 219
Hudson River, 140, 197-208
Hudson River Corridor Act (1965), 205, 206
Hudson River Valley Commission, 205-208
Hudson River Valley Commission Act (1966), 206
Humboldt State Redwood Park, Calif., 178

Ickes, Harold L., 190
"Inholdings," 34, 40-50, 70, 228
Interior, U. S. Department of, 6, 14, 15, 16, 21, 25, 97, 99, 175
Iowa, 144-154
Iowa Conservation Commission, 145-149
Izaak Walton League, 4, 199

Jackson, Glenn L., 126
Jackson, William Henry, 75-76
Jackson Hole area, 51-60
Jackson Hole National Monument, 52-55, 59
Job Corps programs, 6
Johnson, Andrew, 13
Johnson, Robert Underwood, 36

Kennedy, Ed, 213
Kent, William, 186
Kipling, Rudyard, 6, 73

Land and Water Conservation Fund, 109-111, 113, 147-148
Land and Water Conservation Fund Act (1965), 109-110, 147
Land Management, Bureau of, 25, 97-105, 115, 121, 127
Lane, Franklin K., 23, 187

Las Trampas, N. M., 174-178
Last Landscape, The (Whyte), 142
LeConte, Joseph, 26
Leopold, Aldo, 77
Lewis, Meriwether, 152-153
Lewis and Clark Trail Parkway, 152-153
Lobbyists, anti-conservation, 9
London, Jack, 73

Marshall, Robert, 77
Martin, Carmel, 211
Mather, Stephen T., 22-24, 40, 42-46, 118, 186, 187
McDuffie, Duncan, 192
McFarland, Horace J., 36
McGee, W. J., 17
McKinley, William, 13
Merriam, John C., 186, 187
Merrill, Bill, 40
Metropolitan Museum of Art (New York City), 181
Minneapolis, Minn., see Twin City Metropolitan Area
Minnesota, 129-143
Mississippi River, 153
Monterey Coast Highway Study Commission, 211
"Monterey County Coast Master Plan," 211-223
Monterey County Planning Commission, 211, 212, 215-216, 219
Monterey Peninsula Herald, 213
Monuments, National, 52-54, 186, 224
Movement, conservation, beginning of, 12-25
Muir, John, 26-31, 33, 36-37
"Muir Woods," Calif., 186
"Multiple use," 17, 56, 64-71, 82, 228
Munsey, Frank, 150
Murie, Olaus, 59-60

National Lewis and Clark Commission, 152

National Park Service, 3, 6, 7, 21-25, 39-44, 47, 48, 52, 54-58, 60, 109, 118, 127, 131, 176, 177, 180, 186, 190, 195
National Parks Association, 199
National Parks Magazine, 124
National Wilderness Preservation System, 72, 76
Nature Conservancy, 199
Nelson, DeWitt, 149
New England Wild Flower Preservation Society, 170
New Hampshire, 155-170
New Hampshire Everlasting and Unfallen (Bruns), 156-157
New Hampshire Natural Preserves Forum, 170
New Hampshire Natural Resources Council, 166, 169-170
New Hampshire Water Resources Board, 167, 168
New Mexico, 174-178
New York Herald-Tribune, 150-151, 203, 204
New York Times, 42-44, 46-48, 159, 181, 203, 204
Noble, Maud, 57
North Cascade Range, 229

Ochs, Adolph S., 181
Olmsted, Frederick Law, Jr., 138, 182-184, 192-193
Olmsted, Frederick Law, Sr., 193
Olney, Warren, Sr., 33-35, 37-38
Olney, Warren, III, 3
Oregon, 113-128, 138, 154
Oregon Highway Commission, 115-117, 119, 120, 126-127
Osborn, Henry Fairfield, 186, 187
Outdoor Recreation, Bureau of, 101, 106-113, 152
Outdoor Recreation Resources Review Commission, 67, 106-107
Owings, Nathaniel A., 175, 177, 212, 215, 218, 219

Owings, Mrs. Nathaniel A., 215

Parks
  National, 18, 21-24, 32-36, 39-50, 51-60, 61, 74-76, 100, 112, 148, 224, 226, 228, 230
  regional, 106-113
  rural, 129-143
Peekskill Evening Star, 204
Penny, J. R., 103
Pigeons, passenger, 5
Pinchot, Gifford, 4, 14-17, 20-23, 28, 36, 62-64, 71, 99-100, 115, 117-118, 161, 162
Pittman-Robertson Act, 146
Policies, conservation, 7, 17, 20, 82
Pollution, water, 7, 124-125, 126, 167, 168
Pomeroy, A. Watson, 203
Portland Oregonian, 118-119
Post, Bill, 211
Prairie Creek State Redwood Park, Calif., 178-180
Projects, conservation, difficulties of promoting, 8-11
Public Land Law Review Commission, 99
Public Roads, Federal Bureau of, 172, 173
Public Sales Act (1964), 99

Rainbow Natural Bridge, 74
Rainier, Mount, 75
Raymond, Randall P., 168
Recreation areas, 2, 4, 7, 9, 10, 21, 22, 57, 62-71, 82, 83, 99-113, 182-184, 224, 227
  Iowa and, 144-154
  Minnesota and, 129, 131-134, 138, 142
  New Hampshire and, 155, 169
  Oregon and, 113, 124-127
Redwoods, 4, 5, 25, 178, 179, 185-196, 209, 210, 212, 227
Reserves, forest, 16-20, 25

Richardson, Governor (Calif.), 192
Roberts, John L. D., 211
Rockefeller, John D., Jr., 48, 49, 56-58
Rockefeller, Laurance S., 106, 205
Rockefeller, Nelson, 203-206
Rockefeller Forest, 4
Rollins, Frank W., 158
Roosevelt, Franklin D., 52, 53
  Darling, Jay N., and, 151
Roosevelt, Theodore, 4, 9, 13, 14, 20-21, 61, 64, 71, 115, 162, 186, 187
  Darling's cartoon of, 151
Ross, H., 212
Rousseau, Jean Jacques, 73
Rural Area Development projects, 6

St. Paul, Minn., see Twin City Metropolitan Area
San Francisco, Calif., Hetch Hetchy Valley issue and, 30-38
Santa Fe Trail, 153
Save-the-Redwoods League, 4, 25, 163, 185-195, 228
Scenic areas, preservation of, 1-2, 7, 21, 22, 27, 28, 36, 44, 48, 49, 53, 56, 61, 66, 68-69, 74-76, 79, 81, 100, 104, 106, 178, 180, 182-183, 199, 202-207, 213, 215-216, 221-222, 224, 225, 228, 229
  Iowa and, 152-154
  Minnesota and, 138-139, 142
  New Hampshire and, 155-170
  Oregon and, 114-128
Scenic Hudson Preservation Conference, 199, 201-202, 208
Sempervirens Club, 186
Service, Robert W., 73
Sequoia National Park, 2-3, 50
Sequoias, 26, 29, 193
Sierra Club, 27, 28-29, 33, 35, 37, 189, 199, 228
Sierra range, 26-38, 39-40

Skidmore, Owings and Merrill (architectural and engineering firm), 212, 215
Snake River Land Company, 57
Society for the Protection of New Hampshire Forests, 156-159, 162-164, 166, 169
Soil Conservation Service, U. S., 167
Spaulding, Roland B., 158
Speaker, E. B., 149
Spell of the Yukon, The (Service), 73
Sport Fisheries and Wildlife, Bureau of, 109
Sproul, Robert G., 187
Squam Lake, N. H., 166-168
Standard Oil Company, 57
Stevens, Lawrence N., 108-109
Storm King (mountain), 197-208
Sundry Civil Bill, 20
"Sustained yield," 65

Taft, William Howard, 159
Teton Mountains, 51-60
Thomas, Lowell, 205
Time (magazine), 220
Transportation, U. S. Department of, 175, 176
Tuolumne River, 34
Turner, Frederick Jackson, 73
Twin Cities Area Metropolitan Development Guide, 139-142
Twin City Metropolitan Area, 129-143

Udall, Stuart, 124, 126, 152
Umpqua River valley, 120-121
"Use Book," 16-17

Vanderbilt, Commodore, 213

Wapiti, see Elk
Wapiti Wilderness (Murie), 59
Waste, 7, 30, 125
Water pollution, 7, 124-125, 126, 167, 168

Watersheds, protection of, 4, 17, 65, 99, 100, 194-195

Weeks, John W., 159-161

Weeks, Sinclair, 160

"Weeks Law," 159-162

Wegener, John, 40

Wheeler, Benjamin Ide, 187

White, John R., 2-3, 80

White, Stewart Edward, 73

White Mountain National Forest, 155, 160, 162

Whitney, J. D., 31

Whitney, Mount, 31

Whyte, W. H., 106, 142

Whyte, W. H., Jr., 205

Wilbur, Ray Lyman, 49, 187

Wilderness Act (1964), 66, 76-80

Wilderness areas, preservation of, 18, 72-83, 155-156, 224, 225, 226

Wilderness Preservation System, National, 72, 76

Wilderness Society, 4, 199, 228

Wildlife, conservation of, 3, 5, 22, 62, 65, 137, 146, 147, 151, 152, 224, 225, 227

Willamette River Park System, 123-126

Wilson, Woodrow, 35

Wirth, Conrad, 131

Wirth, Theodore, 130-131

Wisconsin, 153

Wynant, John G., 158

Wyoming Game and Fish Commission, 55

Yellowstone National Park, 50, 61, 74, 75-76, 153, 158, 230

Yosemite National Park, 2, 23, 30, 31-32, 34, 36, 39-50, 61, 75, 76, 153, 158, 230

Young, C. C., 192

Zoning, 8, 102, 136, 142, 215-216, 218, 220, 230